TBN SPECIAL EDITION

RIGHT PEOPLE RIGHT PLACE RIGHT PLAN

DISCERNING THE
VOICE OF GOD

Expanded
Edition

JENTEZEN FRANKLIN

WHITAKER
HOUSE

RIGHT PEOPLE, RIGHT PLACE, RIGHT PLAN:
DISCERNING THE VOICE OF GOD
(TBN SPECIAL EDITION)

Jentezen Franklin Ministries / Kingdom Connection
P.O. Box 315
Gainesville, GA 30504
www.jentezenfranklin.org

ISBN: 978-1-64123-075-9
eBook ISBN: 978-1-60374-143-9
Printed in the United States of America
© 2017 by Jentezen Franklin

Whitaker House
1030 Hunt Valley Circle
New Kensington, PA 15068
www.whitakerhouse.com

1 2 3 4 5 6 7 8 9 10 11 ⨆⨆ 25 24 23 22 21 20 19 18 17

DEDICATION

This book is dedicated to the six darlings in my life:
my wife, Cherise, without whom I would be nothing;
my four daughters, Courteney, Caressa, Caroline,
and Connar; and my son, Drake.
May the lessons in this book be a part of
the spiritual legacy
I leave behind for all of you.

APPRECIATIONS

A special thanks to three of the greatest men of God I have ever been privileged to know: Tommy Tenney, T. F. Tenney, and Steve Munsey. Their mentorship in my life has been profound.

To my congregation at Free Chapel, which has loved, supported, and believed in me for so many years, I want to express my sincerest gratitude.

Lastly, a special thanks to my television partners, who enable me to take the gospel around the globe.

CONTENTS

PART I

THE GIFT OF DISCERNMENT

1

YOUR INTERNAL COMPASS

Man shall not live by bread alone;
but man lives by every word that proceeds
from the mouth of the LORD.
—Deuteronomy 8:3

In the middle of China, an ordinary person repeatedly drops a small shard of iron onto a leaf and watches as the leaf floats on the water. Inexplicably, the leaf spins around until it points in the same direction every time. Historians and archaeologists now believe that this is how the compass, the original navigational tool, was discovered—years before the Bible was ever written.

They had no concept of north and south—the alignment naturally sought by the metallic shard—and for millennia no one would discover why this solitary piece of metal behaved as it did. Yet, years later, the compass would be embraced by sailors and travelers needing the precise direction to lead them to their ultimate destination. Before the compass, these wanderers could only look around and set their course by the physical markings around them. They had no idea that there was an internal force—in this case, the earth's magnetic field— that influenced that small piece of iron.

Inside every believer, ordinary and extraordinary, there is a compass—an internal force—placed by God, waiting to be discovered and used for His glory. When you learn to utilize and trust this valuable resource, you will find that you can better navigate the stormy seas and cloudy skies of life.

Whom should I marry?

What will I do with my life?

Do I take this job?

Should I invest my money in this opportunity?

Inside every believer, ordinary and extraordinary,
there is a compass—an internal force—placed by God,
waiting to be discovered and used for His glory.

Life, it seems, is a never-ending cycle of decisions that can alter the entire direction of our lives. How freeing it would be if we had access to an internal compass that would fix the direction of our lives to true north. Without it, we are left to look around and set our course by the markings of our physical world—our emotions, hunches, and the voices of those who would want to influence our journey.

What if we could learn to rely on the compass set in place by our creator? What if we could discern the voice of God in our lives? God desires to speak into your life, if only you would learn to recognize His voice. By the power of His Holy Spirit, He has given you all you need to set the course of your life that will lead you to the right people, the right places, and the right plan in order to achieve His perfect will for your life.

THE VOICE OF GOD

In Genesis, God said, "Let there be," and there was! The heavens, the earth, the land, and the seas were all spoken into existence by the voice of God. Then we read: *"God said, 'Let Us make man in Our image, according to Our likeness'"* (Genesis 1:26). Thus, man was made in the image of God, who then put His life within man, *"And the LORD God formed man of the dust of the ground, and breathed into his nostrils the breath of life; and man became a living being"* (Genesis 2:7). As the image of God, man was different from the rest of creation for he was a self-determined being. Man had a voice in how his life would turn out. He was created in the likeness of God.

Man demonstrated this immediately as he began to name the animals. Just like his Creator, man could also talk and call things by a name. Man was not a god himself, but he could speak like God, and Godlike force was in his voice because God had *"breathed into his nostrils the breath of life."* God breathed His voice into Adam.

But Adam and Eve were not alone in the garden. Satan slithered in and immediately went to work driving a wedge to separate man and woman from the voice of God. Notice his approach: *"Now the serpent was more cunning than any beast of the field which the LORD God had made. And he said to the woman, 'Has God indeed said?'"* (Genesis 3:1). Satan knew that if he was going to defeat the human race, he had to separate man from the voice of God. You know the rest of the story. Satan said, *"In the day you eat of it your eyes will be opened, and you will be like God"* (Genesis 3:5). Does anything strike you as strange there? How about the fact that they were already like God! They had been created in the likeness of God.

Satan knew that if he was going to defeat the human race, he had to separate man from the voice of God.

Here we get a sneak peek into the strategy of the enemy in your life: he will do whatever he can to get you to listen to his voice instead of the voice of God. He would like nothing better than to suggest the direction of your life. He will tell you that you have to be someone else—someone other than who God wants you to be. Why else would he suggest to Eve that she could *"be like God,"* implying that Eve was not already made in the likeness of God? Perhaps that is why so many people spend their whole life trying to impress others by being something that they are not. Their lives are racked with frustration and regret. They don't understand that God made them to be themselves—made in His image. You don't have to be somebody you are not—you are already what He wants.

In 2007 I experienced what can only be described as a divine encounter. I had just finished a television taping in Orange County, California, and was driving down Jamboree Boulevard to have dinner with a friend of mine. As we drove, we passed a large building with a huge cross in front and I asked him whose church it was? He told me the name of the pastor and I asked him to turn around immediately. I didn't know why at the time, but God was putting me in the right place to launch a miraculous plan.

The pastor of that church, Floyd Lawhon, called me the week before. He's an old friend whom I've known for many years and he was letting me know he was retiring from his church in Southern California and returning to the East Coast. Once inside we were greeted by some men who told us that Floyd had already moved and that we had just missed him. As we walked through the building you could sense the enormous potential. I was so moved that I called Floyd on the cell phone and I said, "I cannot believe what you've done in Southern California! God has used you to do an amazing work here!"

Then I asked him, "What's going to happen to the church now that you've retired?" After a pause his voice broke as he said, "I can't believe you've called me." He said, "I believe you're supposed to have a part in that building." He went on to say, "I was supposed to tell you this last week when we spoke, but I didn't have the nerve. It sounded so farfetched!"

I didn't know what to say at the moment so I told him I would pray about it. We looked around the building and as we were about to leave, one of our hosts asked if we would pray for his seventeen-year-old son. I will never forget what happened next. This man's son had been fasting for three days for God to send the right pastor to that church. I can tell you right now that messed me up.

I went back to the hotel room and immediately called Cherise. She agreed that we would fast and pray and seek God's will. To make a long story short, within months, Free Chapel OC was birthed and, as this book is being written, we just celebrated ten years at our Irvine campus. It wasn't without its obstacles, and Satan did all he could to keep us from God's plan, but ten years later we know why. Every week altars are full of people accepting Jesus Christ as Savior and experiencing His love and mercy for the first time. Thousands of people gather at the OC campus weekly to encounter the living presence of God and discover His purpose for their lives!

I didn't know at the time why I felt impressed to turn around and go to that church. But I've learned, when being sensative to the Holy Spirit, to be obedient. Your obedience will open doors you may not even know existed and can provide more confidence for even greater things to come. The OC campus turned out to be our first multisite campus. We now have five campuses in three different states and an online church that reaches thousands every week.

Learning to be sensitive to the voice of God is critical to every facet of your life, but obedience when you actually hear from God is the real test. Can God trust you with what He says to you? Will you trust Him when you cannot see His hand at work, and then move forward, believing that through your obedience you too can stand in miracle territory?

After the fall, God came walking through the garden in the cool of the day. What did Adam and Eve do? They hid from the voice of God. From that moment on, the Old Testament becomes a chronicle of mankind's love/hate relationship with the voice of God.

In Exodus, God spoke with Moses through a burning bush and, later, dictated the Ten Commandments until the mountain they stood upon shook. The people told Moses, "*You speak with us, and we will hear; but let not God speak with us, lest we die*" (Exodus 20:19). Look at how well Satan's plan was working. Man went from speaking with God in the garden to being afraid of His voice. Satan had so perverted man's relationship with God that they thought the very sound of His voice would kill them. Today, his plan is no different. He will convince you that if you listen to God, it will kill your relationships, your career, and your fun. He will tell you that the Word of God will take life from you.

Eventually, things got so bad that God said, in effect, "Okay, you don't want to hear My voice anymore? You don't want Me to speak to you? Fine. I'm done." With that, His Word stopped. Scripture ceased—bringing an abrupt end to the Old Testament.

And for four hundred years, the voice of God was silent.

Satan will convince you that if you listen to God,
it will kill your relationships, your career, and your fun.
He will tell you that the Word of God will take life from you.

Eventually, that silence was broken by "*the voice of one crying in the wilderness*" (Matthew 3:3). The book of John leaves no doubt that God was ready to speak again: "*In the beginning was the Word, and the Word was with God, and the Word was God.… And the Word became flesh and dwelt among us*" (John 1:1, 14). God had broken the silence, and now His voice had skin and bones.

When Jesus started His ministry by being baptized in the Jordan River, God could hold His tongue no longer: "*And suddenly a voice came from heaven, saying, 'This is My beloved Son, in whom I am well pleased'*" (Matthew 3:17).

Can't you just imagine the demons trembling? The voice that was in the garden, the voice that walked "*in the cool of the day*" (Genesis 3:8), that voice was back on the planet speaking into the lives of His beloved creation. The Word of God was back to display its power. Jesus spoke to a storm and it stopped. Jesus spoke to Lazarus and he walked out of a grave. Jesus spoke to a fig tree and it withered. When His followers expressed amazement at the demise of the tree, Jesus informed them, "*Assuredly, I say to you, if you have faith and do not doubt, you will not only do what was done to the fig tree, but also if you say to this mountain, 'Be removed and be cast into the sea,' it will be done*" (Matthew 21:21).

It was official. Not only was God's voice active again, but it was also free to work within those who called upon Him. God was not finished working through the lives of His people. In fact, He was just getting started.

GOD'S VOICE IN YOUR LIFE

How can you discover that special, internal direction that God uniquely gave to you? What is God's plan for your life? Most women today can feel anything but special as they try to fulfill the ever-present demands of career, church, and family. They feel left out, stressed out, and frazzled. Most men today are confused as the world tries to feminize them, and then expects them to be "real men" by satisfying their every desire. They feel marginalized, emasculated, and under attack.

God sees you as extraordinary, and He desires to use you in extraordinary ways. He is searching for men and women who dare to believe they can make a difference. Today, the body of Christ (the church) must open up their spiritual ears to hear and recognize the voice of the Almighty. Could it be that God wants to use you as a key player in His kingdom in these last days?

I was six years old, taking a bath with my G. I. Joe action figures one Saturday night, when I began to sing Bill Gaither's song, "The King Is Coming." My mother, who was listening, entered the bathroom and said, "Jentezen, our church musicians are out of town tomorrow and your dad asked me to take care of the music. I have everything lined up but the special music for the offering. Will you sing that song tomorrow for the offertory?" She kept on pushing me, not taking no for an answer.

"I will if you pay me twenty dollars," I finally said.

"It's a deal!"

My mother read between the lines, hearing something about her son's destiny through her spiritual discernment. Neither one of us knew that singing that song the next day would launch me into my ministry.

Believe it or not, I still remember that day. Tears were flowing as the congregation was moved. The tender touch of God came upon my life. Later I began to sing in the choir and play the drums, the sax, and the piano, which led to my accepting the call to preach.

Today, I pastor an amazing church filled with thousands of people, and I reach millions through television and digital media. But it was all triggered by the amazing discernment of my mother.

There are things that you know that you can't explain. First John 2:20 says, *"But you have an anointing from the Holy One, and all of you know the truth."* All believers have an anointing, a spiritual touch of God, that provides them with remarkable insight.   Through the Holy Spirit, from whom flows all the gifts, graces, and superior knowledge of God, you have inside information on what God's will is.

God has given every ordinary believer an extraordinary gift. He has given you an internal compass to guide and discern things about your children, your spouse, your family, your career, and your finances.

This discernment is not from human wisdom; it is from God. In the next few chapters, you will learn how to:

+ activate the voice of the Holy Spirit.

+ trust your inner voice of discernment.

+ apply that discernment in everyday life.

+ make a profound difference in your loved ones' lives by just being you.

As you will soon see, this will be the most important life lesson you've ever experienced as you fulfill your assignment in becoming the man or woman God created you to be.

Take a moment now to stop and reflect on what you have read, and what it means to you and for your life. Consider each of the questions below and journal your answers. Date this page, so that when you look back, you will have a record of your journey in this season of life. Any time the Lord speaks to you, it is important to record it.

DATE: _____

CHAPTER 1 QUESTIONS:

1. Give a brief summary of your reading from chapter 1.

_____

_____

_____

_____

2. List two key points that stood out to you.

_____

_____

_____

_____

3. Describe the last time you heard the voice of God speak into your life.

_____

_____

_____

_____

4. Describe how the voice of God spoke into your life through chapter 1.

_____

_____

_____

_____

5. Explain your understanding of the term "internal compass."

_____

_____

_____

_____

6. Based on what you have learned in this chapter, are there any areas of your life in which you will begin to act or think differently?

_____

_____

_____

_____

CHAPTER 1 CONCLUDING REFLECTION

Your reflection should include the following:

+ What you learned

+ What had the most value for you or had direct application to your life

+ Any other takeaways

_____

_____

_____

_____

_____

_____

_____

_____

_____

_____

_____

_____

_____

_____

_____

_____

_____

_____

_____

_____

2

A FEEL FOR THE REAL: DISCERNING GOD'S VOICE

They should seek the Lord,
in the hope that they might grope for Him
and find Him, though He is not far from each one of us.
—Acts 17:27

Have you ever been reading a book at home near a light when a little moth flitted by you? You barely noticed it; it's a tiny little insect.

Did you know there is only one time in Scripture where God is compared to a moth? The prophet Hosea pastored God's people during one of the most prosperous eras of Israel. Eventually, in the midst of all their prosperity, Israel began to backslide, and Hosea warned them, *"Therefore I [God] will be to Ephraim like a moth"* (Hosea 5:12). But just two verses later, he says, *"For I [God] will be like a lion to Ephraim"* (verse 14). Hosea's prophecy to Israel reveals a great concept about discernment. It demonstrates how God speaks to His people.

If you will be receptive and obedient to the Holy Spirit's voice when God wants to guide you, He will never hit you with anything more powerful than a moth. However, if you are insensitive and resistant to His voice, He will come to you like a lion. God is so gentle. His first choice in getting your attention is to come to you like a moth. He doesn't want to have to roar like a lion. If you opened your closet door and a little moth was flying around the light bulb, you might not even notice it. But if you opened your closet door and were greeted by the roar of a lion, that would probably get your attention.

It's a beautiful thing to be gently led by the Holy Spirit. As feathery as a moth, God is trying to direct you and show you His way; His preference is not to resort to the lion to chase us in the right direction—but He will. *"I will return again to My place till they acknowledge their offense. Then they will seek My face; in their affliction they will earnestly seek Me"* (Hosea 5:15).

When we don't follow the gentle leadings of the Word of God and of the Holy Spirit, we then grow insensitive to His presence. Insensitive people wait for the lion to come before they will believe God is telling them anything. Some people say, "Well, if God doesn't want me to do it, then He needs to send something to stop me." Again, God's desire is to use the gentle leadings of the Holy Spirit (the moth), but if we remain stubborn or insensitive to this, He will get our attention one way or the other (the lion).

A dramatic example of this moth/lion approach is found in 2 Samuel. King David's rebellious son, Absalom, sent for Joab in order to send him with a message to his father. But Joab would not come. Absalom sent for him a second time, but still Joab would not obey. Finally, Absalom sent his servants to set Joab's barley fields on fire. With his fields burning, Joab came running to Absalom and asked, "Why have your servants set my field on fire?" Absalom replied, in effect, "I sent for you once, then sent for you a second time, and still you didn't come. So, I set your barley fields on fire as a last resort to get your attention." (See 2 Samuel 14:29–31.)

A FEEL FOR GOD'S VOICE

By now you are probably wondering, *How do I activate this discernment in my life? How do I recognize the prophetic whispers of God?*

I once heard about a US Treasury officer who had the job of identifying counterfeit dollar bills. He said, "The key to identifying a false bill is to spend hours and hours handling the real thing." In other words, you have to get a "feel for the real" if you want to identify the fake.

As you spend time with God praying and studying His Word, you will develop a feel for the voice of God. You will instantly begin to recognize when something does not feel right in your spirit.

In Genesis 27, Isaac could have avoided being deceived if he had had a "feel for the real." Jacob, Isaac's younger son, wanted the blessing that belonged to his older brother, Esau. In order to get it, Jacob had to convince his father to speak the blessing over him. So, Jacob's mother, Rebekah, came up with a clever scheme to fool the aging Isaac, whose eyesight was beginning to fail. Jacob mimicked Esau's voice and covered his arms with animal pelts in order to disguise himself as his older, and more hairy, brother. By pretending to be Esau, Jacob deceived his father and obtained the blessing that was traditionally reserved for the firstborn child. (See Genesis 27:22.) Slightly suspicious at this strange sounding voice, Isaac felt Jacob's arm to assure himself that this was, in fact, Esau. Notice, the old man could have discerned the fraud if he had trusted his ears. We must be careful because often the voice of error can sound nearly identical to the voice of truth.

People often mistake other voices for God's voice.
The gift of discernment separates the false voices from the real.

You have to learn to trust your spiritual ears. Jesus said, "*The sheep follow him, for they know his voice*" (John 10:4). Isaac knew something wasn't right when he heard Jacob's voice. He felt Jacob's arm and was deceived by the hairy texture. But spiritual truth cannot be judged by outward circumstances. Although Isaac was old enough to recognize deception, we need to realize that we are never too old to be deceived. We will never get to the place where we don't have to fine-tune our spiritual sensitivity. You need to handle the Word of God enough to know truth from error.

People often mistake other voices for God's voice. The gift of discernment separates the false voices from the real. Some things just don't feel right. It doesn't necessarily mean God is not speaking to you, but if there is a reservation in your spirit, you should wait for God to give you the green light and confirm your feelings before proceeding.

If you feel that something is not right, it could be that it is not according to God's timing. The prodigal son would have gotten his inheritance without experiencing any sorrow if he had waited on his father's timing. Acts 17:27 says, "*They should seek the Lord, in the hope that they might grope for Him and find Him, though He is not far from each one of us.*" Just like the counterfeit money handler, we can become so familiar with the voice of God that we are able to immediately recognize the counterfeit voice of Satan when we hear it.

FALLING FOR THE COUNTERFEIT

Have you ever thought you heard God tell you something, only to find out later that you didn't hear from God at all? Until you learn to accurately discern God's voice, you're bound to have a few mistakes.

Years ago, I suffered a humbling experience in this area. My wife and I had gone out for the evening. We left the kids at home with strict instructions about what was permissible and what was not. As it was Christmas time and a lot of candles were sitting around the house, one of the instructions was not to play with matches. We were very clear: there was to be no lighting of candles.

When we arrived home from our evening out, we were shocked to discover that some of the candles had been burned. We knew this because the guilty party left a trail of melted wax on the hardwood floors. I quickly called the kids in for a lineup and interrogation.

"Who lit these candles?" I asked.

They all denied it. I explained that if they confessed, their punishment would be less severe. Still, no one admitted it. I then went down the list of names one by one. "Did you do it?" All five children denied any involvement. My wife and I knew one of them was not telling the truth. We asked them repeatedly, but still no confession. We were beginning to get upset, not so much because of the candles, but because we knew one of them was flat-out lying.

The atmosphere grew more intense by the minute. We warned the kids of the dangers of lying, and I preached every sermon I knew on the subject. By the time I got through with my little lecture, I had them all dangling by a thread over the hot flames of hell! Repeatedly, I warned, "This is your last chance. Who did it?"

To our amazement, only silence filled the room. But we weren't done. Our next tactic was to separate the kids; hoping one of them would crack and "rat" on the guilty one.

After talking to each of the kids, it became apparent that our oldest daughter was skirting the truth. We zeroed in like two hardened, NYPD detectives. We peppered her with one question after another trying to obtain a confession, or at least to blow her flimsy story out of the water.

Although her story stayed the same, so did the mask of guilt she wore on her face. I was convinced she was lying to me. Finally, we got the break in the case we'd been looking for when her sister, Caroline, entered the room. She said, "Just admit it, Courteney. I didn't see you burning the candle, but I saw you watching TV in that room and touching the candle."

At last, an eyewitness! To our amazement, she still denied it. Finally, being the all-wise father, I pronounced judgment, "Courteney, you don't have to admit it. I feel in my spirit that you did it. I feel like God has revealed to me that you're the one."

I gave her a spanking and sent her to her room. Before she left the room I warned her, "Courteney, you can't fool the Holy Spirit. You can fool your parents, your teachers, and other authority figures, but you can't fool God. He always knows the truth."

Caroline came to us an hour later in tears. She admitted, "I did it, I'm sorry. I didn't want to get in trouble. It was me!"

The entire family gathered to remind me that I had just spanked an innocent child, and even worse, I did it because I felt God was telling me she was guilty.

"I thought you felt it in your spirit, Dad," one of them said. From across the room, another one accused, "Yeah, Dad, God told you to whip the wrong kid, right?"

I apologized to my daughter. I was sorry I had misjudged her, and I told her the discipline would count as a credit for her in the future. I was fairly sure she would need it one day. As for Caroline, let's just say that her conscience felt better, but her bottom didn't. Over the years, this incident has become one of the family jokes that we still laugh about today. But it serves as a reminder that discerning the voice of God may take some trial and error.

Have you ever experienced anything like this? Maybe you have started a business or a ministry venture and really put yourself out there only to find that, what sounded like a good idea, wasn't God's plan for your life. This can be embarrassing, or even worse, demoralizing. Whether it's a failed relationship, a bad investment, or fill in the blank, you have to know that ultimately the Lord orders the steps of a righteous man or woman. It's your heart and your willingness to stop, look to God, and surrender all over again that will open the door, or open your eyes, to what God has for you to do next. There will be a "next," and this time, you will be wiser. This time, you will not make the same mistakes you made the last time.

THE INNER PERSON

There are so many voices in the world. There is the voice of God, the voice of the devil, the voice of people, and your own inner voice. How do you discern between God's voice and all the others? How do you know the difference between a word from the Lord and too much pizza or, even worse, gas?

The Bible tells us, *"God is not the author of confusion"* (1 Corinthians 14:33). In the Old Testament, it was easy. Whenever God wanted the Israelites to go in a certain direction, He just moved the cloud that guided them. When the cloud moved, they moved. When the cloud stayed, they stayed. (See Numbers 9:21–22.)

It is a little more complex today. The cloud of the Old Testament has moved within. *"The spirit of a man is the lamp of the* LORD, *searching all the inner depths of his heart"* (Proverbs 20:27). The way God speaks and leads us is through our spirits. We have to be spirit-conscious in order to hear God's voice and receive His direction. First Thessalonians 5:23 says, *"May the God of peace Himself sanctify you completely; and may your whole spirit, soul, and body be preserved blameless at the coming of our Lord Jesus Christ."* We are a spirit, living within a body, and we possess a soul, which is our mind, will, and emotions.

The way God speaks and leads us is through our spirits.
We have to be spirit-conscious in order to hear
God's voice and receive His direction.

In the Old Testament, God dwelt within a temple with an outer court, an inner court, and a holy of holies. But under the new covenant, He has a people for His temple. Our body is the outer court, our soul—or mind—is the inner court, and our spirit is the holy of holies. God now dwells in a three-room house: body, soul, and spirit.

When God leads you, He does so not by your carnal mind or by your flesh, but by your spirit. When you are born again, your spirit is born again. Ephesians 3:16 says, *"that He would grant you...to be strengthened with might through His Spirit in the inner man."*

First Peter 3 speaks of the hidden person of your heart, *"Rather let it be the hidden person of the heart, with the incorruptible beauty of a gentle and quiet spirit, which is very precious in the sight of God"* (verse 4). Therefore, we have this hidden, inner person, someone living inside of you. It is your eternal spirit. But, because your inner spirit is born again, it is more finely "in tune" with God's Spirit than is your flesh. You can't make your inner person enjoy sin. If you start to do something wrong, your inner voice will say, "Hey, what are you doing up there? I'm down here, and I don't like that."

YOUR SPIRITUAL ALARM SYSTEM

Before you were born again, it never bothered you to do certain things; but now that you are born again, God is residing within your inner man and is making you like Jesus. Your spirit connects with God and has a voice, and you need to start listening because your success depends not by being led by your mind, your emotions, or your flesh, but by your spirit.

God has placed some indicators—almost like a spiritual alarm system—within our spirits. Here are five indicators you need to recognize in order to discern God's voice.

1. YOUR SPIRIT CAN BE STIRRED.

In Acts we read, *"Now while Paul waited for them at Athens, his spirit was provoked within him when he saw that the city was given over to idols"* (Acts 17:16). Notice it wasn't necessarily Paul who was stirred up and provoked, but his spirit.

Does God ever stir you up about something or somebody? Maybe it's a friend you haven't seen or someone you haven't thought about in a long time, but God begins to stir the person up in your heart. Sometimes, that is God's voice speaking to your spirit, urging you to reconnect with that person because He needs you to minister to him or her. Similarly, He can use these stirrings to show you a place to go, a task to complete, or a calling for your life.

2. YOU CAN BE LED BY YOUR SPIRIT.

In Romans it says, *"Those who are led by the Spirit of God are sons of God"* (Romans 8:14). Sometimes, God will give you *leadings* within your spirit. When your spirit is led, the Holy Spirit is urging you to do something. When you are Spirit-conscious, God can use you to do great things, whether it is sharing the gospel with a receptive listener or sending twenty dollars to someone you just feel might need it. We are reminded over and over in Scripture to pray in the Spirit, to be led by the Spirit, and to listen to the Spirit. Being sensitive to the voice of the Holy Spirit is the secret to knowing God's next steps for your life. There is simply no other shortcut. He will use His Word, His church, His people, and everything around you to help you hear clearly what He has planned for you. You just have to take the time in your busy world to sit before Him and listen.

Being sensitive to the voice of the Holy Spirit is the secret to knowing God's next steps for your life. There simply is no other shortcut.

---

3. YOUR SPIRIT CAN HAVE PURPOSE.

Returning to Acts, it says, *"When these things were accomplished, Paul purposed in the Spirit, when he had passed through Macedonia and Achaia, to go to Jerusalem"* (Acts 19:21). Paul purposed, not in his mind or in his flesh but *"in the Spirit."* In John 4:24 it says, *"God is Spirit, and those who worship Him must worship in spirit and truth."* We connect with the Spirit of God directly through our spirit, not through the flesh and not through the soul or mind. Therefore, if you are going to do what God wants you to do, you must purpose it in your spirit, not in your mind or emotions. If I purpose in my flesh to worship God, then I won't do much worshipping. If I purpose in my flesh to go to church, then I won't go very often. But when I purpose in my spirit to worship God, it gets my unwilling body out of bed and focuses my unruly mind on God once I get to church.

When we started building our new worship facility, I purposed in my spirit that we were going to build it. Usually there is a time of divine misery before there is a divine change. I remember feeling urgency about the building program. I began to receive scriptural confirmation and a stirring in my spirit that God was saying, "Now is the time to build."

Some people said we could not do it; however, when purpose gets in your spirit, all things are possible. You have to purpose in your spirit, which is connected to the Spirit of God. You can't let your flesh or your mind tell you what you're going to do. You must purpose in your spirit to obey the voice of God and do what He has called you to do.

4. YOU CAN BE BOUND IN YOUR SPIRIT.

Acts 20:22 declares, *"And see, now I go bound in the spirit to Jerusalem, not knowing the things that will happen to me there."* Paul's spirit was bound to Jerusalem. He didn't know if he would be welcomed or rejected—it didn't matter. When God wants to put you somewhere, He binds you in your spirit to that place.

I'm bound in the spirit to the church that I pastor; I'm bound in the spirit to my wife. When God binds you in the spirit, it is very difficult to leave because your spirit is tied to that place or person. Don't ever let your mind or emotions make you walk away from something to which God binds you in spirit. Stay the course and don't quit. Don't give up, because you might miss out on God's mighty plan.

Don't just go to any church; let God bind you in your spirit to a place. Places matter—God created places before He created people. God specifically created the garden of Eden for Adam and Eve and placed them there. (See Genesis 2:7–8.) Many people have location frustration; they're in the wrong place. Let God bind your spirit to the right place, the right people, and the right plan for your life.

5. YOUR SPIRIT CAN GIVE YOU PEACE ABOUT THE RIGHT DIRECTION.

Second Corinthians 2:12–13 says, *"Furthermore, when I came to Troas to preach Christ's gospel, and a door was opened to me by the Lord, I had no rest in my spirit."* Just because a door is wide open doesn't mean you're supposed to walk through it. This is where you need the Holy Spirit's guidance. Do you realize that if Paul had continued to go in the direction he was going, toward Asia, he might never have gone to Macedonia and to Rome? Thus, Europe, the United States, and the Western world would not have received the gospel when they did and may have even remained pagan.

The door was wide open, but Paul said, "*I had no rest in my spirit.*" Sometimes, determining God's will is this simple: if you don't have rest in your spirit, don't do it. A lack of divine rest in your spirit is usually God's way of saying no.

If you don't have rest in your spirit about a relationship or a major decision that you're about to make, then I encourage you to give yourself some time to pray. "*Whoever believes will not act hastily*" (Isaiah 28:16). I have learned that God is always right. If I follow His urging, He never misleads me. Remember, God has promised to give wisdom to His children if they will seek it. (See James 1:5.) His desire is that you would hear His voice.

Take a moment now to stop and reflect on what you have read, and what it means to you and for your life. Consider each of the questions below and journal your answers. Date this page, so that when you look back, you will have a record of your journey in this season of life. Any time the Lord speaks to you, it is important to record it.

DATE: _____

CHAPTER 2 QUESTIONS:

1. Give a brief summary of your reading from chapter 2.

_____

_____

_____

_____

2. List two key points that stood out to you.

_____

_____

_____

_____

3. What kinds of struggles do you have when it comes to "discerning God's will" for your life?

_____

_____

_____

_____

4. Describe how the voice of God spoke into your life in chapter 2.

_____

_____

_____

_____

5. Based on what you have learned in this chapter, are there any areas of your life in which you will begin to act or think differently?

_____

_____

_____

_____

CHAPTER 2 CONCLUDING REFLECTION

Your reflection should include the following:

+ What you learned

+ What had the most value for you or had direct application to your life

+ Any other takeaways

_____

_____

_____

_____

_____

_____

_____

_____

_____

_____

_____

_____

_____

_____

_____

_____

_____

_____

_____

_____

3

THE NOD OF GOD: DISCERNING GOD'S WILL

In all your ways acknowledge Him,
and He shall direct your paths.
—Proverbs 3:6

Is this God's will or not?

This is a question you will have to confront on more than one occasion in your lifetime. Just as we can develop ears to recognize God's voice, discernment to know God's will is also available to the believer. I call it "the nod of God," when you feel a divine yes on the inside about something.

In Numbers 22, Balak tried to bribe Balaam, the prophet, to curse the Israelites. Balaam asked God if he should do it. When God told him no, Balak tempted Balaam with more money. A word to the wise: never move simply for more money. Balaam went back to prayer and asked God a second time to let him curse Israel. No matter how much money was involved, God would not change His mind.

Balaam, who I'm sure could have used the cash, was trying to talk God into doing his will instead of doing God's will. This reminds me of how many people make decisions that do not have the nod of God on them. They try to get God to bless the decisions or relationships when He has already said, "No, I don't believe that choice is right for you. I have someone better for you." Like Balaam, we sometimes go back to God, trying to change His mind. But God has made it clear, *"For I am the* Lord, *I change not"* (Malachi 3:6 kjv). If God doesn't change, guess who *is* going to have to change?

Too often, we fail to ask God how He feels about our relationships, our financial investments, and the major decisions we make. I once wanted to buy a house in a great subdivision. I could just see our family living there, but when I prayed about the house, it seemed as though heaven's phone number was unlisted. Even though I told God what a good buy the house was, and what a great investment it would be for us, I could not get the nod of God to purchase that house. I might add that my wife sided with God and did not think the house was right for us either.

I kept going back day after day and asking God in prayer for peace about buying the home, but I just couldn't get a peace about it. Disappointed, I passed on purchasing the house. A few months later, I learned it was badly in need of major reconstruction. If I had not listened to the voices of God and my wife, that house would have cost me tens of thousands of dollars.

Proverbs 3:6 says, "*In all your ways acknowledge Him, and He shall direct your paths.*" Your part is to acknowledge Him; His part is to direct your path. You may really want to buy that new car or house, but pray about it first and wait for the nod of God. Here's a tough question to ask yourself whenever you bring a decision before God: *are you willing to hear Him say no?*

Balaam kept asking God repeatedly to let him go, until God said, in effect, "All right, if you want to go, then go." It reminds me of my son asking, "Daddy, can I go outside and play?" I would say, "No, it's bad weather outside; you can't go." Five minutes later, he would be back, pleading, "Daddy, Daddy, can I go now? Can I? Huh? Please, please, Daddy." At some point, I got so worn down and so tired of being asked, that I would say, in frustration, "If you want to go so badly, then go." In reality, I was not giving my permission; I was saying, "I dare you." I knew that if he went out in bad weather, he would suffer the consequences. He would probably catch a cold.

In the same way, God said to Balaam, "If you want to go, if you insist on going over My will, then go." Here's a frightening truth: there comes a time when, if you keep on stubbornly persisting about something that does not have the nod of God, He might just let you have it—literally. This always leads you down a painful road.

Balaam rode off on his donkey to curse Israel, but God put an angel in his path to try and stop Him. Balaam's donkey saw the angel in the middle of the road, but the prophet didn't. Sometimes, we can't see what we should, but God is gracious enough to surround us with those who can, until we can see it for ourselves. Have you ever been so headstrong, so outside of the will of God, that nobody could reason with you? The donkey was Balaam's friend, but Balaam beat the animal mercilessly because it would not continue to support him in going against God's will. Then, God supernaturally opened the mouth of the donkey and allowed it to speak to Balaam.

This had to be the world's most unusual conversation. Can you imagine these two donkeys talking to one another? One of them was a four-legged donkey, and the other was a two-legged donkey. The strange thing was, the four-legged donkey was the smarter of the two.

Balaam continued to kick and beat the donkey. In reality, he should have been kissing that donkey because it was trying to save his life. When we are stubborn and out of God's will, sometimes we kick and mistreat the well-intentioned. Young people kick their parents and embrace destructive friendships. Husbands and wives kick their spouses while they embrace destructive and divisive relationships.

Eventually, Balaam saw why the donkey was trying to turn him around. When you go in a direction that does not have the nod of God, sooner or later, you will see that God's way was the right way. You should immediately double back, swallow some pride, and thank all the people who had the courage to tell you the truth. Even when you were blinded by lust or selfishness, God was faithful to put people in your path who tried to stop you from walking off that cliff.

I don't want to be like Balaam, a fool on a mule on the road to destruction. If I'm getting ready to mess up my life, I want God to stop me. When you wait for the nod of God before acting, it's like an early warning system that detects the enemy's mines and missiles before they are visible to the natural eye. From years of experience, I have learned to heed God's warnings. Every time I have brushed them off as merely being a case of indigestion or a mere coincidence, I have regretted it later. When you're about to make a major decision and you feel a "check in your spirit," or have a sense that something is wrong, you better heed the warning and wait for the nod of God.

There comes a time when, if you keep on stubbornly persisting about something that does not have the nod of God, He might just let you have it—literally.

When you have God's approval on your decisions, He will provide everything you need to do His will. Don't ask how much it costs; ask if God wants it done. If it's God will, then it's God's bill! Where God guides, He also provides. What God initiates, He will orchestrate. John 10:14 says, *"I know My sheep, and am known by My own.*" His sheep recognize and follow the familiar voice of their Shepherd. They refuse to follow a stranger's voice.

How do the sheep know the Shepherd's voice? Through daily communion with the Shepherd. We must cultivate the ability to discern the voice of the Holy Spirit. When our relationship is distant, His voice seems muted. However, God will always hear us when we call, no matter how far away we've wandered. I know the voice of my children. I can be at a busy mall and hear other voices all around me, but when I hear one of my children say "Daddy," even in the midst of all the clutter, I instantly recognize that voice.

RACING AHEAD OR BEING LED

The problem is, we don't spend enough time with God to recognize His voice when He speaks. You cannot raise a family successfully without the voice of God leading you in wisdom. You cannot run a Christian business without the voice of God giving you direction. There is a vast difference between being led and racing ahead. When we don't hear Him, we find ourselves running at break-neck speed, confused and unproductive, always pushing and driving.

Are you racing ahead or are you being led? Your spirit wants to lead you; your flesh wants to race ahead like a toddler loose in a parking lot. The flesh thrives on noise, activity, competition, and busyness; the spirit thrives on silence, stillness, solitude, and Scripture. *"Be still, and know that I am God"* (Psalm 46:10).

A few years ago I participated in a mission trip to the Ukraine, where our church supports an orphanage in Kiev. While touring the orphanage I noticed a beautiful little eight-year-old girl. She stuck to me like glue. Every time I preached in the city at different churches, if she was there, she would come up and give me a hug. She truly captured my heart.

I went home and told my wife about her. I showed her pictures and, after much prayer and seeking God's will, we decided to pursue adopting the child. We were told it would be a relatively quick and easy process. Nothing could have been further from the truth.

We made numerous attempts to work out the adoption, including trips to the Ukraine where we met with government officials. We used all the contacts we had in that nation, as well as contacts within the States, but to no avail. Nothing we did brought us any closer to adoption. After two and a half years of emotional highs and lows, we finally realized that we were racing ahead in our own desire, rather than being led by the Spirit of God. It was one of the most painful times in our family's history.

When you try to force things to happen, it's almost always a sign that you are racing ahead, and not being led. As Psalm 23:2 reminds us, *"He leads me beside the still waters."* The whole time we were trying to adopt the little girl, we didn't have peaceful, still waters in our home. We had turmoil and confusion. We may never fully understand everything that happened during that season of our lives, but we have realized that being led by God brings peace, while racing ahead based on our own will exhausts all our resources.

Your spirit wants to lead you; your flesh wants to race ahead like a toddler loose in a parking lot. The flesh thrives on noise, activity, competition, and busyness; the spirit thrives on silence, stillness, solitude, and Scripture.

THE WORD OF GOD

Jesus spent much time alone with God. If it was that important to the Son of God, there are certainly times when we must be alone with God as well. One of my favorite singers and musicians is Jason Upton. His music is some of the most inspirational that I have ever heard. He and his band go to a monastery every year for three to four days to seek God. During those days, they fast from speech—no sound, no music, no noise at all. In the quiet, God begins to speak. The spirit, you see, thrives on solitude. The voice of God does not scream; it's a still, small voice. In order for you to hear Him, you must learn to get quiet in His presence. You won't learn anything while you're doing the talking.

Many will argue that listening for the voice of God is too hard. When my children were young and still at home, there were seven of us: my wife, four girls, my son, and me. Sometimes, meals would be chaos; bedtimes could be a battle; outings became an ordeal, but they were all a necessary part of everyday life. Spending time with God, although it may be difficult at first, is also a necessary part of everyday life—and one that helps get you through the rest of the chaos.

You have to plan your time with God. Make plans after the kids go to sleep or before they get up. You need those times alone with God so He can speak to you. He will give you confirmation about His will for your life. In order to spend time consistently with God, I set a place and a time for prayer.

God guides us by His Word, which is relevant for all people. Every believer has a right to hear God. Not knowing the Word of God, however, can greatly hinder you from receiving His direction. Psalm 119:105 says, *"Your word is a lamp to my feet and a light to my path."* The Scriptures are the Word of God, which the Spirit of God thrives in. Pour over them, and the Word of God will cleanse you of the world's impurities, wash you clean, and make you more like Christ.

Psalm 32:8–9 says, *"I will instruct you and teach you in the way you should go; I will guide you with My eye. Do not be like the horse or like the mule, which have no understanding, which must be harnessed with bit and bridle, else they will not come near you."* Parents understand what eye contact is with their child. If you can just catch their eye, it's like a telepathic communication. You know what's going on, what they're feeling, what they're planning.

The voice of God does not scream; it's a still, small voice.

In order for you to hear Him,

you must learn to get quiet in His presence.

You can be led by God's eye, or by the bit and bridle. Don't be like the horse or the mule that has to have a bit and a bridle. You're a sheep, not a stubborn mule. Learn to listen to His impressions and wait on the nod of God.

FORCING YOUR WILL

Have you ever tried to put a puzzle together? Sometimes, a puzzle piece can look right, but it doesn't fit properly. It has the right appearance, but it will not fit into the empty space without force. You must never force a piece to fit a space for which it was not designed. Just one misplaced piece destroys the finish. It causes all the other pieces to become disjointed, and it will leave a hole someplace else. Every piece of a puzzle is connected, just like the pieces of our lives. We were created for a particular purpose, and just one piece out of place can greatly affect all the other pieces of our lives.

Don't try to force things to fit. Wait on the nod of God. If you don't have His approval for the direction you're headed, don't force it. God holds the missing piece of the puzzle.

You see, God has a problem: He expects us to realize that He is God, that His ways are not our ways, and that His thoughts are not our thoughts. (See Isaiah 55:8.) God's greatest pleasure is to be trusted.

TWO EXTREMES

Beware of wandering toward two extremes when trying to discern the voice of God. The first extreme is over rationalizing. This is where you only do what is completely logical. Every door must be opened and every question answered before you will make a move. We say to God, "You show first, and then I'll go." But God says to us, "You go, and I'll show." He implores us to *"walk by faith, not by sight"* (2 Corinthians 5:7).

The other extreme is mysticism. To err on this side is to completely ignore reality. Everything becomes "I just felt led," or "God told me." There is nothing wrong with feeling led by God, but too many people use this line as a shield against the advice of others. It signals the end of the conversation.

One of the problems with the SCUD missiles in the first Gulf War was that, even though they were high-powered weapons, nobody knew quite where they were going to land. Being high-powered but misguided can often cause more harm than good.

EXPERIENCING GOD'S GUIDANCE

There are seven ways in which the discerning believer can truly experience God's guidance, and determine God's will.

1. INNER CONVICTIONS

On February 24, 1989, a United Airlines 747 took off from Honolulu, Hawaii, headed for Sydney, Australia. While in flight, the cargo door blew open, sending some of its passengers to a watery grave in the Pacific Ocean. A man named John was on that flight. He spoke about the incident at a Christian business luncheon at our church. He was sitting at the passenger door, when he distinctly heard a voice on the inside saying, "Move from where you are sitting." He delayed, but the inner voice spoke again saying, "Move now!" He moved into the back of the plane and, a few seconds later, there was a gaping hole where he had been sitting.

Miraculously, the pilots were able to land the plane, but unfortunately, several people lost their lives. Although we'll never know why, John's life was spared that day by listening to the voice of God. Through the Holy Spirit, you can know things that you didn't study or train for. You can gain insight into someone's character. You can have a direct line into the wisdom and knowledge of God Himself.

2. SCRIPTURAL CONFIRMATION

Second Timothy 3:16 teaches, *"All Scripture is given by inspiration of God, and is profitable for doctrine, for reproof, for correction, for instruction in righteousness."* Just as a pilot trusts his instruments, God guides us as we trust in His Word and in His Spirit. A good pilot will tell you that when you are in a storm or fog, you must trust the gauges on the flight panel more than your eyesight. When the storm is raging, stick to the gauges! The same is true in spiritual storms. The Word of God will deliver you through the dark clouds of life.

3. PROPHETIC CONFIRMATION

Through the prophetic word of someone else, God can confirm what He has already spoken to your heart. Sometimes He will use prophetic preaching, and it will seem as though the minister has eavesdropped on your life. First Corinthians 12 speaks of the nine gifts of the Holy Spirit. Two of them, the gifts of prophecy and the discerning of spirits, can help you know the right direction from the wrong direction.

4. GODLY COUNSEL

Proverbs 11:14 says, "*Where there is no counsel, the people fall; but in the multitude of counselors there is safety.*" Psalm 1:1 says, "*Blessed is the man who walks not in the counsel of the ungodly.*" Before you make any major decision in your life, open yourself up to feedback from experienced, wise, godly people whom you respect. They are not a substitute for God's voice, but they may help you discover or confirm His leadings.

Just as a pilot trusts his instruments,
God guides us as we trust in His Word and in His Spirit.

---

5. CIRCUMSTANCES

If you are laid off from your job, God may be directing you to another place of employment. In this case, He isn't leading you through prophecy, an internal voice, or an angel, but through your circumstances. There are times when God will allow things to happen in your life in order to get you to move. For example, no money in your bank account may be God's way of urging you to get a job. We certainly are not to govern all of our decisions by circumstances. However, there are times when we must interpret the circumstances of our lives, and then determine what God wants us to do.

6. THE PEACE OF GOD

"*Let the peace of God rule in your hearts*" (Colossians 3:15). Don't enter into a contract or make a decision that robs you of your peace. Even if everything looks good and sounds good, always apply the peace test. It may take some trial and error to master this one, but learning to trust that barometer in your heart will help you to avoid some future hardship.

7. PROVISION

Remember my little saying: "Where God guides, He provides." Where's the provision? This doesn't mean you'll never experience financial challenges, but it does mean that He has already made provision for the vision that He has been putting into motion. *"I have not seen the righteous forsaken, nor his descendants begging bread"* (Psalm 37:25).

In conclusion, I feel it is important for you to realize that, although God chooses any one of these ways to answer our prayers, He may use more than one to confirm His Word. God has told us that two or three witnesses will confirm His Word for us. (See Deuteronomy 19:15 and 2 Corinthians 13:1.) The bigger the decision, the more you will want to confirm His direction through these seven ways.

When you develop the ability to hear and discern God's voice, you will be amazed at how involved He wants to be in your everyday life. Ask God for His guidance; once you get the nod of God on your decisions, everything else will fall into place. *"And thine ears shall hear a word behind thee, saying, This is the way, walk ye in it"* (Isaiah 30:21 KJV).

There is a part of your brain called the reticular activating system. Have you ever bought a car thinking no one in your area owned one, but as soon as you drove off the lot, all you could see were cars just like yours? Suddenly, they seemed to be everywhere! Why didn't you notice them before? Because, after your purchase, your reticular activating system reprogrammed your brain to notice what you hadn't seen before—cars just like your new one.

Even as you're reading this book, God is activating a gift within your spirit called discernment. Maybe before you read this book, you didn't realize it was there. But from now on, it's going to be hard to miss the spiritual intuition God has given you.

I would like to pray into your life the principles we have learned so far:

Father, in Jesus' name, I pray for the man or woman of God who is reading these words. I pray that You will activate the gift of discernment in their lives. May You have full reign of their spirits so they can be stirred by Your spirit, pressed by Your spirit, bound by Your spirit, and have rest in Your spirit. I pray they will recognize the gentle whispers of the "moth" and be led by them. I pray for the nod of God to be on their every decision and relationship. I ask You to give them such a feel for the real that they will not miss Your purpose for any area of their lives. In Jesus' name I ask, Amen.

Take a moment now to stop and reflect on what you have read, and what it means to you and for your life. Consider each of the questions below and journal your answers. Date this page, so that when you look back, you will have a record of your journey in this season of life. Any time the Lord speaks to you, it is important to record it.

DATE: _____

CHAPTER 3 QUESTIONS:

1. Give a brief summary of your reading from chapter 3.

_____

_____

_____

_____

2. List two key points that stood out to you.

_____

_____

_____

3. Chapter 3 asked a critical question: Whenever you bring a decision before God, *are you willing to hear Him say no?*

_____

_____

_____

_____

4. Describe how the voice of God spoke into your life in chapter 3.

_____

_____

_____

_____

5. Based on what you have learned in this chapter, are there any areas of your life in which you will begin to act or think differently?

_____

_____

_____

_____

CHAPTER 3 CONCLUDING REFLECTION

Your reflection should include the following:

+ What you learned

+ What had the most value for you or had direct application to your life

+ Any other takeaways

_____

_____

_____

_____

_____

_____

_____

_____

_____

_____

_____

_____

_____

_____

_____

_____

_____

_____

4

I'M THE ONE, THIS IS THE PLACE,
AND NOW IS THE TIME

Is any thing too hard for the LORD? At the time appointed I will return
unto thee, according to the time of life, and Sarah shall have a son. Then
Sarah denied, saying, I laughed not; for she was afraid. And he said, Nay;
but thou didst laugh.
—Genesis 18:14–15 KJV

Genesis 18 records one of the most significant events in biblical history. In fact, with the exception of the birth, life, death, and resurrection of Jesus Christ, the story of Abraham, Sarah, and their two sons have arguably had the greatest impact on history—especially on the twenty-first century. The birth of Ishmael, the father of the modern-day Muslim faith, and Isaac, through whom the seed of Jesus Christ would come, has become one of the biggest political and religious struggles on earth today.

Before Ishmael and Isaac, there were Abraham and Sarah, two key players, both in their senior years of life, and there was a word from God…a promise. But as God revealed His promise to Abraham and Sarah that day, Sarah's response caught the attention of God, and not in a good way.

"Where is your wife Sarah?" they asked him. "There, in the tent," he said.
Then one of them said, "I will surely return to you about this time next
year, and Sarah your wife will have a son." Now Sarah was listening at
the entrance to the tent, which was behind him. Abraham and Sarah were
already very old, and Sarah was past the age of childbearing. So Sarah
laughed to herself as she thought, "After I am worn out and my lord is old,

will I now have this pleasure?" Then the LORD *said to Abraham, "Why did Sarah laugh and say, 'Will I really have a child, now that I am old?' Is anything too hard for the* LORD? *I will return to you at the appointed time next year, and Sarah will have a son." Sarah was afraid, so she lied and said, "I did not laugh." But he said, "Yes, you did laugh."* (Genesis 18:9–15 NIV)

Sarah laughed and said, "Will I really have a child, now that I am old?" In other words, Sarah pronounced herself "unfit" and beyond anything God could do because of her advancing years and the advancing years of her husband. From that day forward, she would, time and time again, circumvent the plan of redemption, the plan of the ages, and limit what she deemed possible to what she could see in the natural. She thought she wasn't the right person, that it wasn't the right time, and that it wasn't the right place.

Many people, like Sarah, take a step back when confronted with something amazing God wants to do in their life. Like Sarah, far too often the response is, "I'm not the one, this is not the place, and now is not the time." When we limit what can happen to only what we *think* is possible, we completely eliminate God from the equation, and we restrict our purpose to only what is possible in the natural. Why do we do this? We say God can do anything, but our thinking and our actions tell a different story about what we really believe.

Let me start by laying out a few basic truths: First, you are the one. Second, this is the place. Third, now is the time.

Scripture is replete with people whom God spoke to with a magnificent plan for their life, and yet their response was always the same: they only saw impossibility when God showed them what was possible.

When we limit what can happen to only what we think *is possible, we completely eliminate God from the equation, and we restrict our purpose to only what is possible in the natural.*

First, there is Moses in the desert. A bush catches fire but is not consumed, and then the bush starts talking. Within seconds Moses knows exactly who it is that is speaking to him. It is the Lord God, the Almighty. You can almost hear the tremble in Moses' voice when God says, "I've chosen you to do something magnificent." Moses responds, "Who am I? And who shall I say sent me? God, I'm slow of speech." He's throwing all of these excuses at God. (See Genesis 3–4.) Moses had a speech impediment, and, after forty years, he had pretty much given up on any possibility of doing anything other than tending sheep and being a good husband and father. What he's saying is, "I'm not the one, this is not the place, and now is not the time." But Moses was wrong, and so are you when you throw up excuses and reasons to avoid that still small voice calling you to *your* purpose.

I thought about Gideon, in a cave hiding at a time when the nation needed a great leader. The Bible says that the angel came and said, "You are a mighty man of valor." And Gideon replied, "But I am the youngest from the smallest tribe and I'm poor. I don't have anything. Are you hearing me, God? I'm the least of my brothers." (See Judges 6:12, 15.) In other words, get someone else to do it! In essence, Gideon was saying, "I'm not the one, this is not the place, and now is not the time." But God saw it differently. What I love about Gideon is that, even after his vehement protest, when God finally and emphatically made it clear that he *was* the one, Gideon's response was surrender. His response was, "I am the one, this is the place, now is the time." (See Judges 6:17.) After several cuts to the team, Gideon, with three hundred men, defeated the mightiest war machine on the planet at that time. Gideon surrendered to the call of God and solemnly acknowledged, "I'm the one."

I challenge you, right now, wherever you are reading this book, to say these three words out loud: "I'm the one." Say it again with some force: "I'm the one!"

TIME TO STAND UP

On a cool September afternoon in 1779, John Paul Jones was fighting for the American colonies. He got in his little ship and sailed into the North Sea only to be overwhelmed by a fleet of British warships. Those warships began to fire their great cannons across the bow of his boat, and Jones knew that if he didn't surrender, his little ship would be blown out of the water. So, at their direction, he pulled up next to a huge British battleship and they tied his ship to theirs. The British captain, with a callous attitude and a condescending voice, asked Jones, "Do you surrender?" John Paul's response: "Surrender? Why I have not yet begun to fight!" Three hours later, he had so defeated the British that their captain turned his ship, his soldiers, his guns, and everything he had over to John Paul Jones. With that brave stand by the captain of one small ship, Jones struck a lasting blow to the forces of tyranny.

After I read this story, I remember thinking, *If the human spirit of one man with that kind of resolve can fight and win against those kind of odds, what could God do if we would take seriously what He wants us to do as individuals, as a church, as a people?*

How long will the church keep saying, "I'm not the one; somebody else needs to do something?" When will we start saying, "I'm the one! This is the place! Now is the time!"?

I will never forget January 15, 2009, when US Airways flight 1549 was disabled by striking a flock of Canadian geese after takeoff. The plane immediately lost power, forcing the pilot to attempt a water landing in Manhattan's icy Hudson River . The world watched as the flight crew scrambled to get all the passengers out of the sinking plane only to find themselves struggling to stay alive, fighting hyperthermia, and hoping for a rescue before it was too late. An onlooker on the bridge saw people going under the water, drowning, screaming for help. Without hesitation, this bystander tore off his coat and dove into the frigid waters.

We all watched with rapt attention as he swam over and rescued one woman and her daughter and then swam back out to rescue another person. Then, as if that wasn't enough, he swam back out again. Before it was all over, he ended up saving the lives of five people. TV cameras were there, carrying it live, broadcasting it into the homes of people across the nation. All one hundred and fifty-five people aboard the plane survived.

Unbeknownst to the brave rescuer, there was a young woman who was watching the live newscast of all this in her apartment. She turned to her two little children and said, "That looks like something your father would do." Three hours later she found out that it was their father!

That is the kind of father and mother you want to be when crisis hits. Your family needs to know that you're the person who will stand up and say, "I am the one to do something about this. This is the place and now is the time."

Why do we cower back in the heated and challenging moments of life? Why do we retreat? Why do we shy away from challenges? It's time for us to realize that if anything's going to happen we have to get a revelation of "I'm the one" and "this is my home" and "my family" and "my marriage" and "my kids" and *I can do something about it, through Christ!*" This is the time!

The church of today needs to understand that we are just as called as Jeremiah was when God said, *"Before I formed you in the womb I knew you; before you were born I sanctified you; I ordained you a prophet to the nations"* (Jeremiah 1:5).

In Psalm 139:4–5, David said, "O LORD,… [You have] *laid Your hand upon me.*" This is the same hand that wounded Jacob's thigh, the same hand that brought down the walls of Jericho, the same hand that parted the Red Sea, and the same hand that raised the dead, fed the five thousand, and healed the sick. The same hand!

That hand is upon me right now. That hand is upon you. We can make a difference in our nation, in our cities, in our communities, and in our families. We must stop saying, "Somebody needs to do something, somewhere." We need to start saying, "I'm the one, this is the place, and now is the time!"

You have ears that have twenty-four thousand fibers that vibrate each time someone is speaking to you, giving you the ability to hear. It's what helps you hear the tide coming in, the music of an opera, or the chirp of a robin's song outside your window.

We must stop saying, "Somebody needs to do something, somewhere."
We need to start saying,
"I'm the one, this is the place, and now is the time!"

You have a body that has five hundred muscles, two hundred bones, and seven miles of nerve fiber, all synchronized to give you agility and movement. You have a heart that will beat thirty-six million times this year, allowing it to pump six hundred thousand gallons of blood to sixty thousand miles of blood vessels, veins, and arteries. You have lungs that have six hundred million pockets of folded flesh that expunge gassy waste from your system so that you can live, breathe, and stay alive. You have five quarts of blood, and in those five quarts of blood you have twenty-two trillion cells. Within each cell are millions of molecules. Inside each molecule is an atom, and those atoms oscillate. Every second that ticks off, two million cells in your body die, and two million more cells are produced. You are a walking resurrection, even while you read this book!

You have a brain that is three pounds of gray matter. It has four million pain sensors, five hundred thousand touch detectors, and two hundred thousand temperature gauges that make sure you don't overheat or freeze.

If God would invest that much in a body that will decay, die, and go back to dust, I wonder what He has put in our spirit that is eternal and will last forever! You are the one! God has invested a lot in you!

At some point, you need to say, "I'm the one, this is the place, and now is the time. And through Christ, I can make a difference in my world!" I believe this about you. God knew you would read this book before I ever penned one word.

REWRITING YOUR LIFE STORY

There was a Swedish chemist who picked up the newspaper the morning after his brother had died. Only the newspaper columnist had the story wrong. The newspaper reported that *he* had died, not his brother. When this chemist saw his own name in the obituary column, he noticed that while they had the wrong brother's name, the obituary was truly an accurate synopsis of his life and his achievements. The newspaper had written this: "He invented dynamite and he left a legacy of enabling the nations of the world to reach new levels of mass destruction. He will always be remembered as 'the Merchant of Death.'" After reading this obituary, the man declared, "I will not leave that kind of legacy." He took the millions of dollars he had made by helping the nations of the world to blow each other up, and put it in a trust fund. His name was Alfred Nobel, and that trust fund has funded what is now known as the Nobel Peace Prize. Each year, the prize of one million dollars is given to a nation or person who advances the cause of peace in the earth in an extraordinary way. Today, nobody thinks of Mr. Nobel as being the inventor of bombs and dynamite. Everybody thinks of him as a person who advance the cause of peace through the Nobel Peace Prize trust fund.

What am I saying to you? I'm saying that you can turn your life around today. What would *your* obituary read today? Whatever it is, there is still time to rewrite it with the help of Jesus Christ. You can make a difference. You can change your direction. You can redirect the trajectory of what your legacy will be.

I don't know what you've done up to this time. You can't redo or undo what has already been done. But, in Jesus' name, you can say, "I'm the one, this is the place, and now is the time." You *can* change the rest of your story.

On July 1, 1776, the first vote on the Declaration of Independence was taken. There were eight states for it, two states against it, and the Delaware vote was split—one delegate for it, one against it and the third was sick in bed at home. John Hancock announced that a final vote would be taken the next day and that the vote had to be unanimous—every state had to vote yes—or else the effort to establish a new nation would be abandoned. Unanimity is tough to achieve in any vote, in any era of history. They knew that Delaware's three votes were essential to the cause. A decision was made to summon the sick delegate who lived eighty miles away.

A rider rode through the night and arrived in Delaware around midnight on July 2. The delegate, Caesar Rodney, was suffering from many ailments, including asthma and cancer of the jaw. After convincing Rodney to come, the rider got the sick man on his horse and began the return journey just as a terrible rainstorm set in. The roads were a muddy quagmire. They had to dismount in several places and walk the horses through the mud. They walked and rode all night long. Finally, in the morning, fresh horses were provided and they rode hard all the way to Freedom Hall in Philadelphia. When he finally arrived, Rodney was so sick and so weak from the journey that they had to carry him into the chamber. As they settled him into his seat, John Hancock asked him, "How say you?" Time stood still, awaiting this singular vote that would alter the course of world history. Rodney did not know that every other state had voted for independence. Only the Delaware vote remained split, which meant his single vote would determine whether or not a nation would be born or aborted.

A hush fell over the room as Rodney spoke: "I vote for independence." And at that moment, and with a loud cheer, his single vote sealed the union that we now call the United States.[1]

You need to understand: that one man could have said, "I'm not the one. This is not the time. And this is not the place." But he didn't. And neither should you.

How long are we going to let people die and go to hell all around us? How long are we going to let kids in school die and go to hell? At some point, some teenager, some youth, some mom, some dad, some businessperson, some church in your city must say, "I am the one. This is the place. Now is the time!" It's so easy to think that God's going to do something in distant places, but the Bible tells us, "*Now is the day of salvation*" (2 Corinthians 6:2). And this is the place!

When God was leading Cherise and me to come to Gainesville, Georgia, to lead at Free Chapel, we felt the Lord saying, "This is the place." I could have looked at it and said, "Atlanta's a lot more fruitful than this place." And many people said that exact thing to me as they tried to talk me out of it. But the Lord said, "This is the place!" Now, some twenty-eight years later, we have five campuses, an international television ministry, and believe the best is yet to come.

We need to wake up to what we have at hand. We need to stop saying, "If I could only go there" or "If only I could do this." Look at what you have right now in your hand. You *are* the one. This *is* the place, wherever your "this" is. And lastly, now *is* the time.

Ecclesiastes says, "*A living dog is better than a dead lion*" (verse 9:4). Do you know what that means? That means that as powerful as a lion is, if he's dead, he is a lost opportunity. This is the day! I'd rather be "*a living dog*" than "*a dead lion*," because it's over for the lion. But if there's life in that living dog, I have a chance! A present opportunity plagued with problems is better than an awesome opportunity that has passed. There are miracles now! Now is the time! We spend too much time lamenting the past and not enough time looking at what we have right now.

Israel refused to march into the Promised Land because they listened to ten spies. Moses tried to intervene for them and asked God to pardon the people, but God said, "You're too late. I'm not going to use you. I've already chosen another generation to enter the Promised Land." (See Numbers 14:18–23.) They missed

---

1. "Founding Father Caesar Rodney: Who He Was And Why He Matters Today," RedState.com, January 15, 2010, http://www.redstate.com/diary/cityonahillpolitics/2010/01/15/founding-father-caesar-rodney-who-he-was-and-why-he-matters-today/ (accessed August 9, 2017).

it by twenty-four hours! "Now is the time!" Did you know that, you can miss your destiny if you wait until it's too late? You can miss your purpose? You can miss the plan that God has for your life? "Now is the time. Today is the day."

When are we going to quit saying, "One day, we're going to do something," "One day, we're going to make a difference," "One day, we're going to really win the world," "One day, we're going to change our nation," "One day, we're going to influence this country for God?" And when are we going to say *"Now is the time!"* This is the moment! This is the place! There'll never be a greater time to give your best, to give your all, to pour your life out on Him than right now.

Right outside of a little country town in North Carolina, there's a little spring of water that comes up out of the ground and trickles out for ten miles. It flows down into the Nantahala River. Then it gets a bit wider, but even there, you can find places where you can run and leap over it. But then it keeps flowing from that river to another river, and from there it flows into an even larger river, and ultimately it flows into the mighty Mississippi River. If you want to cross it there, you have to get on a bridge that's made of stone and steel. The Mississippi River flows into the Gulf of Mexico, and then if you want to try to cross it's too late. You can't cross that! The point is that the time to cross the river is before it gets too wide. It starts out so small, like a conflict in your marriage, or disagreement with a friend or family member. At some point, it would be so easy just to step over and reconcile things. But if you let it keep going, the river gets wider and wider. And before you know it, you're so far apart that there's no way to get back together.

The same is true in your relationship with God. It's so easy at first to get back to God. But the longer you stay in sin, the longer you live in that addiction or iniquity, the wider the gulf between you and God. And before you know it, you're so far apart that it feels like you just can't get back to Him.

That's why Scripture says, "Today is the day of salvation. Now is the time!" There are things you can do today that you may not have a chance to do tomorrow.

God is saying, "The conditions are just ripe enough for another Joshua, another Sarah, another Moses, another Gideon, someone who will say, 'I'm the one, this is the place, and now is the time.'" Throw your hands up. Say, "God, I surrender to Your will. Use me, take me, and anoint me. Let Your will be done in my life."

You can't do anything about your past, but you can rewrite the rest of your life. It starts right here. You're the one, this is the place, and now is the time.

Take a moment now to stop and reflect on what you have read, and what it means to you and for your life. Consider each of the questions below and journal your answers. Date this page, so that when you look back, you will have a record of your journey in this season of life. Any time the Lord speaks to you, it is important to record it.

DATE: _____

CHAPTER 4 QUESTIONS:

1. Give a brief summary of your reading from chapter 4.

_____

_____

_____

_____

2. List two key points that stood out to you.

_____

_____

_____

_____

3. Describe how the voice of God spoke into your life in chapter 4.

_____

_____

_____

_____

4. Based on what you have learned in this chapter, are there any areas of your life in which you will begin to act or think differently?

_____

_____

_____

_____

5. Is there something you feel drawn to or something you believe God is calling you to do?

_____

_____

_____

_____

6. If you knew God was calling you to something, would you do it now?

_____

_____

_____

_____

CHAPTER 4 CONCLUDING REFLECTION

Your reflection should include the following:

+ What you learned
+ What had the most value for you or had direct application to your life
+ Any other takeaways

_____

_____

_____

_____

_____

_____

_____

_____

_____

_____

_____

_____

_____

_____

_____

_____

_____

_____

PART II

RIGHT PEOPLE, RIGHT PLACE, RIGHT PLAN

5

RIGHT PEOPLE

There is a friend who sticks closer than a brother.
—Proverbs 18:24

Have you ever given your best in a relationship, and gotten the worst in return? Remember the lyrics of the popular country song, "Lookin' For Love" by Johnny Lee:

Lookin' for love in all the wrong places,
Lookin' for love in too many faces.

That has become a theme song for far too many people.

It's time to put a stop to getting burned. It's time to start enjoying the healthy, balanced relationships everyone wants and needs. God wants to help you make wise choices about the people you let into your life, everything from friendships to business partnerships to romance. Finding the proper people is an important part of determining God's will for your life.

If you have ever been used, abused, abandoned, or taken advantage of in a relationship, this chapter is for you. Too often, good people get entangled in bad relationships, with disastrous results.

CHARACTER DISCERNMENT

Character discernment is a valuable tool for avoiding toxic entanglements. It is a skill many of us lack. What is character discernment? It is simply the ability to find relationships that are good for you, and to avoid those that are not.

The apostle Paul said, *"You ran well. Who hindered you from obeying the truth?"* (Galatians 5:7). Notice he says *who*, not what. Romans 8:5 says, *"Those who live according to the flesh set their minds on the things of the flesh, but those who live according to the Spirit, the things of the Spirit."*

When some people come into your life, they don't just bring their bodies—they bring their spirits. There are two kinds of people: "flesh people" and "faith people."

Flesh people tear you down and feed your fears, while faith people build you up and feed your faith. Flesh people waste your time and drain your energy. Often, Christians find themselves in confusing relationships that drain them of their emotional energy and greatly reduce their effectiveness. Think of the personal pain that could be prevented if we knew how to avoid unhealthy relationships. This doesn't necessarily mean "flesh people" are bad people; it just means they don't belong in your inner circle. It also doesn't mean that you should shun such people; God wants us to love all those we come into contact with. But we have to make sure that we are surrounding ourselves with more people who fill our lives than drain our lives. One of the first warning signs of spiritual failure is when we begin to isolate ourselves from Christian friends and from the house of God.

Faith people are the kind who fill your life. They draw you closer to being the person God created you to be. They are the ones who will be lovingly honest with you. They are strong when you are weak.

If God wants to bless you, He will send a person; and if Satan wants to curse you, he will send a person. That's why every day we need to pray for 20/20 discernment in the world of the spirit to know the right people from the wrong people.

PAUL: THE PEOPLE WHO LIFT US UP

When Paul needed to be saved, whom did God send? Ananias was the right man in the right place at the right time. (See Acts 9:10–18.) That's what I call a "Kingdom Connection," people God puts in your life who act like a bridge to get you where you're supposed to go. How would you like some Kingdom Connections in your life and career?

The early church rejected Paul because he had persecuted Christians before his conversion. The disciples were afraid of him, so God once again sent a person: Barnabas. Barnabas used his influence with the disciples to get Paul's foot in the door of the church.

When Paul was discouraged, God sent Titus to encourage him. Have you ever had a discouraging day until one person shared some kind words and completely changed your mood? In 2 Corinthians 7:6, Paul said, "*Nevertheless God, who comforts the downcast, comforted us by the coming of Titus.*"

RUTH: THE PEOPLE WE MARRY

Marriage is one of the most important decisions you will ever make. It is a commitment for life. It affects every other area in your life: your future children, where you live, your finances, where you go to church, and so much more. God has a plan for the people you associate with in your dating life. You will be better off if you take the time to be sure that the one you marry is the one who is ordained by God.

Does God care if you are single, widowed, or divorced? Does He notice when everybody goes home together, but you go home alone? You bet He notices! In the book of Ruth, we see the God who said, "*It is not good that man* [or woman] *should be alone*" (Genesis 2:18), step into the shadows of Ruth's life and give her a Kingdom Connection. Ruth's husband had died and she had little prospect of finding a good man. But God didn't send her a loser or a reject. He didn't send her a smooth-talking "player" who would break her heart. He sent her a man who was capable and could care for her. He sent her Boaz.

Boaz was a bit older than Ruth was, but he had enough money to make her comfortable. Notice the qualities that you should look for, or teach your children to look for, when trying to discern the right mate. Boaz was a stable man. He wasn't just out of prison or rehab. Nor was he lazy and unproductive.

Notice also that he was respectful to Ruth's relatives. He gave Ruth food to take home to her mother-in-law, Naomi. Boaz paid the bill; they didn't "go Dutch." These days, men don't seem to understand how to respect a woman and show respect to her parents. Ladies, if you are dating a guy who reluctantly pays for the meal on the date, but expects you to pay for the movie and the popcorn, then you're dating a deadbeat. Take notes here, gentlemen. Boaz was a man's man—a perceptive man, a sensitive man, a spiritual man, and a financially capable man. That's an equation that equals a *husband!*

Sitting still and waiting is the hardest thing to do.

This actually means you will have to trust God in the matter.

When Ruth came home loaded with food, Naomi began to mentor her on how to conduct herself in a proper way. When Ruth wanted to know what she should do about this man showing her romantic interest, Naomi gave her some sound advice: "*Sit still, my daughter, until you know how the matter will turn out*"

(Ruth 3:18). "Sit still and wait." In other words, "Let the man pursue you; don't pursue him." Today, the girl would call back in thirty minutes saying, "Do you remember me, Boaz? I met you in the field." The next morning she would be calling again. "Do you remember me? Can we go out on a date sometime?" Men lose respect for desperate women. Sitting still and waiting is the hardest thing to do. This actually means you will have to trust God in the matter. Even if you're camping out by the phone, waiting on him to call, don't let him know it. Sit still and wait! Ruth could have reacted selfishly and told old Naomi, "You don't know what you're talking about. Just because you lost your husband doesn't mean that I'm going to lose a chance at a second one." But she didn't. The Bible said she obeyed and respected Naomi's advice.

Boaz arranged a legal wedding and became her "kinsman-redeemer." They had a son named Obed. Obed had a son named Jesse. Jesse had a son named David, who became a king. David had a descendant named Mary. And Mary had a little child that she named Jesus.

Through Ruth's character discernment, God not only blessed her with a fantastic husband, but He also placed her in the genealogy of Jesus Christ. (See Matthew 1:5.)

JONAH: THE PEOPLE WHO TAKE US DOWN

We need God to restore discernment within us, so we can recognize the right people, the blessed people, the faith people, the Kingdom Connections He has for each one of us. But we also need discernment to recognize the wrong people.

God sent Jonah on a mission to Nineveh. But Jonah disobeyed God's will and headed in the opposite direction to Joppa, where he boarded a ship for Tarshish. During the voyage, the ship he was on ran into a storm that threatened to capsize it. Jonah 1:5 says, *"The mariners were afraid."* Many of us have heard the story of Jonah in sermons and Sunday school lessons, but have you ever stopped to consider the fact that there were other people besides Jonah on the boat about to lose their lives? All it takes is one rebellious, disobedient man to take a whole shipload of people down with him

This is an important lesson for those trying to learn discernment. There are times when you are not the problem. The problem may be the people with whom you're associating. The mariner's boat was taking on water, everyone on board was terrified for their very lives, and it wasn't their fault. They were in the wrong place, at the wrong time, with the wrong person—Jonah.

The mariners were feverishly crying out to their gods. They were casting off supplies, sacrificing their needs to lighten the load. But Scripture tells us that *"Jonah had gone down into the lowest parts of the ship, had lain down, and was fast asleep"* (Jonah 1:5). Sometimes, when your life is rocking and reeling in the storm, it's because of people to whom you have attached yourself!

There are times when you are not the problem.
The problem may be the people with whom you're associating.

Finally, the mariners woke Jonah up from his sleep and asked him, *"What shall we do to you that the sea may be calm for us?"* (verse 11). Jonah answered them, *"Pick me up and throw me into the sea; then the sea will become calm for you. For I know that this great tempest is because of me."* (verse 12). Jonah knew he was the problem. So, why would he ask them to cast him over? Why not just jump off the boat?

Sometimes, rebels try to make you feel bad. If you have a forty-five-year-old son who won't get a job, is still living at home eating your food, and is not paying rent, then it's time to throw Jonah off the boat! When you do, don't be surprised if he tries to make you feel guilty for doing the right thing. I can just hear his pitiful words, "You're right; I know I should do better. I'll just find somewhere else to stay. I guess I could sleep at the bus station."

We can wander into storms simply by trying to help people by doing for them what they should be doing for themselves. If the mariners had not tossed Jonah off the boat, everyone would have perished. If you have people in your life who are using you for a free ride, they're not going to voluntarily jump off the boat. If you have relatives or friends who play on your conscience and goodwill to get you to pay their bills or give them money, do you think they're going to stop? If you have a husband who physically abuses you or has affairs on the side and you allow it, you are giving him a license to treat you like a dog.

The Bible says that before they threw Jonah off the boat, they tried rowing harder to bring the ship to land. We often try to work the problem harder because we are afraid of the decision we know we are going to have to make. We try so hard to reap success out of sin. Finally someone on the boat called a business meeting. They took a vote and decided to throw Jonah off the boat. I'm sure the mariners felt bad about it, but they knew that, if they didn't, they were not going to make it to the other side. The Bible continues, *"So they picked up Jonah and threw him into the sea, and the sea ceased from its raging"* (Jonah 1:15). As soon as you get the wrong people out of your boat, your storm will cease. You will experience a great calm. Some of you need to throw some Jonahs off your boat!

If you throw a Jonah off your boat, remember that God is still there for him. When they threw Jonah off, God had already prepared a great fish to swallow him and take him to Nineveh, his intended destination. When you allow the wrong people in your life, you're not helping them—you may be keeping them from what God has prepared for them.

Ask God to reveal the Jonahs in your life who are rocking the boat. Pray for the wisdom and courage to "throw" them and all their baggage off your boat! Sometimes, you have to do what is best for you and trust God to take care of the other person.

As soon as Jonah was off the boat, the mariners began to worship God. (See Jonah 1:16.) You cannot worship God as you ought to as long as there are toxic relationships and turmoil all around. Whatever is stealing your peace and rocking your boat, whatever is taking your smile away, reach down, pick it up, and throw it overboard. Then do what the mariners did—start worshiping God.

WHO'S YOUR MENTOR?

One of the secrets of success for some of the great Bible heroes was in their mentors. If you don't have a godly mentor in your life, you need to ask Him to put one there. When He does, don't hang back and wait for the person to approach you; you might need to ask him or her to mentor you. Joshua was always there, standing in the shadows halfway up the mountains, or outside of the tabernacle, hanging out around Moses. Elisha's success was found in his relationship with Elijah. He spent hours and hours learning from the wise old prophet.

The apostle Paul speaks of Timothy, *"a true son one of the faith"* (1 Timothy 1:2). Timothy was one of the youngest apostles in the Bible. How did he succeed at such a young age? He literally sat at the feet of the great apostle Paul and caught his spirit.

Jesus spent three and a half years of His life in ministry. Most of His time was not with the crowds, or with rich and influential leaders, but with twelve men into whom He poured His life and wisdom. He would speak in parables to the crowds of people, then He would explain and elaborate with the disciples. These men became the building blocks of His church.

Mentors expose you to new orbits of ministry, new habits, and new levels of expectation. Ask the weightlifter or the track-and-field high jumper what a coach does for them. If you want to be the best, the mentor will keep raising the bar, asking for a little more effort and for better results, and teaching you to expect more from yourself.

At times, mentors may even seem cruel and inconsiderate, but if you want to be a winner, their coaching can urge you to the top. Proverbs 27:6 says, *"Faithful are the wounds of a friend, but the kisses of an enemy are deceitful.*" It's a great day when God gives you someone who loves you enough to put you under a little pressure so you can be conformed into the image of Jesus Christ and reach your highest potential.

If you want to be the best, the mentor will keep raising the bar, asking for a little more effort and for better results,
and teaching you to expect more from yourself.

BEWARE FALSE BRETHREN

If you have spent your life gravitating toward all the wrong people, I have good news for you. God will bring the right people and toss out the wrong people. But when He does, don't return to the wrong people. *"Every branch in Me that does not bear fruit He takes away"* (John 15:2). That does not mean they're inferior and you're superior; it just means they are not a part of God's plan for your life. Like Jonah, God has a different plan, a different course for them. But if you insist on grafting them into your life, God may have to do relational surgery and prune them out.

Unfortunately, such false brethren can sometimes be found within your own family, where it is hard to prune them out. At family gatherings, they often bring condemnation. It was only when the prodigal son failed that he realized what his older brother was made of. Upon his return and repentance, his father did not bring up the sins of the prodigal. It was his elder brother who pointed his finger and condemned the prodigal son to his father. (See Luke 15:11–32.)

Joseph discovered that false brethren never celebrate your dream. Instead of living in God's land of unlimited favor, they live in a "zero sum" mentality where for you to win, they must lose. Your gain is their loss. If you receive blessing, they believe somehow there are less blessings available for them. Joseph's brothers couldn't stand their father's favor toward the young lad so they threw him into a pit and sold him into slavery. (See Genesis 37:24.)

Some people bless you when they come into your life; some people bless you when they exit your life. There are many good people out there. *"There is a friend who sticks closer than a brother"* (Proverbs 18:24). Use every ounce of wisdom and discernment to find such people. If someone is destructive or producing bad fruit in your life, be careful. Keep looking, praying, and seeking until you find the right people, who draw you closer to being the person God intended you to be.

Take a moment now to stop and reflect on what you have read, and what it means to you and for your life. Consider each of the questions below and journal your answers. Date this page, so that when you look back, you will have a record of your journey in this season of life. Any time the Lord speaks to you, it is important to record it.

DATE: _____

CHAPTER 5 QUESTIONS:

1. Give a brief summary of your reading from chapter 5.

_____

_____

_____

_____

2. List two key points that stood out to you.

_____

_____

_____

_____

3. Describe how the voice of God spoke into your life in chapter 5.

_____

_____

_____

_____

4. Who were your "right people?" Who has been the most instrumental in leading you to Christ? What happened?

_____

_____

_____

_____

_____

_____

Consider writing these people a note of gratitude to let them know the impact they have had on your life.

5. Who are the people that have been instrumental in your development as a believer since you first accepted Christ as your Savior?

_____

_____

_____

_____

_____

Consider writing these people a note of gratitude to let them know the impact they had on your life.

6. Based on what you have learned in this chapter, are there any areas of your life in which you will begin to act or think differently?

_____

_____

_____

CHAPTER 5 CONCLUDING REFLECTION

Your reflection should include the following:

+ What you learned
+ What had the most value for you or had direct application to your life
+ Any other takeaways

_____

_____

_____

_____

_____

_____

_____

_____

_____

_____

_____

_____

_____

_____

_____

_____

_____

_____

_____

_____

6

RIGHT PLACE

And He has made from one blood
every nation of men to dwell on all the face of the earth,
and has determined their preappointed times
and the boundaries of their dwellings.
—Acts 17:26

Many years ago, God began to speak to me about this amazing gift of discernment. I had a dream one Saturday night that was so vivid I will never forget it. I dreamed I was attending the funeral of a child. When I walked up to the little casket and looked in, I was devastated to see Caressa, my own daughter, lying lifeless in the coffin. Immediately, I woke up from the dream and awakened my wife. We both began to pray for our family. We wept as the strong presence of the Lord entered our bedroom.

The next morning, still shaken by this experience, I went to church to preach. I preached a sermon I titled "Cancel the Devil's Assignment." At the end of the message, I tearfully told the congregation about my dream. I explained how I believed God was warning me that Satan had targeted our children at a young age, but through the blood of Jesus Christ, we could cancel the devil's assignment in their lives. It was one of the most moving services I'd ever taken part in, as fathers and mothers began to cry out to God on behalf of their families.

This is where the story takes a dramatic turn. Our family had planned to go on vacation to Disney World in Florida the next day. For some strange reason, my wife begged me to leave after the morning services ended. She kept on pleading with me, "Let's go one day early so we can go to SeaWorld tomorrow."

SeaWorld hadn't even been on our itinerary, but I consented, and we arrived in Florida one day early.

The next morning, we took our two daughters to SeaWorld. It was a beautiful, sunny day as we waited for the ski show to begin in the uncovered, five-thousand-seat stadium. Out of nowhere, a huge, dark storm cloud emerged and covered the park. The wind picked up drastically. We heard a clap of thunder when suddenly, right before our eyes, a streak of lightning hit the top of a nearby hotel, setting it on fire. Panic-stricken, five thousand people rushed up the steps of the stadium, seeking shelter from the storm.

Total chaos ensued. Cherise grabbed the diaper bag and accessories while I snatched one of the girls. Our youngest daughter walked up the steps herself. By the time we neared the top of the stadium, thunder and lightning were all around us. Both of our girls were hysterical. To be honest, so was I. Never before had I encountered anything like this. The strong winds triggered my mind to watch for a tornado. When we reached the top of the steps, it was so crowded that Cherise quickly turned to pick up Caressa. But, as she reached for her, Caressa ran right past her to a total stranger standing nearby. The stranger, a twenty-six-year-old woman, reached down and picked up our daughter without hesitation. Caressa wrapped her arms around the young lady's neck and wouldn't let her go.

Of all our children, Caressa was by far the clingiest to her mother; she would never go into a stranger's arms. She always wanted her mother or me to hold her. If she didn't know someone, she wouldn't give them the time of day.

Yet, as Cherise began to plead with her to come into her arms, Caressa wouldn't even acknowledge Cherise or me. She just clung to this woman with all of her might. The lady began to cry—not a tear or two, but uncontrollable sobbing—as she held our three-year-old daughter.

Cherise turned to me and whispered, "Jentezen, do something. This lady is acting weird, and she has our child." I noticed the young woman's mother and father standing beside her, and I saw that her mother was also crying. Now we were totally confused.

My wife gently asked the woman's mother, "Why is everyone crying?"

She responded, "You don't understand. Your daughter is a little angel sent from God to us today."

As the storm started to recede, she began to explain.

"Two months ago, my daughter's three-year-old child died of congestive heart failure in the middle of the night. This is the first time we have been able to get our daughter out of her bedroom because she has been so devastated with grief. She's been blaming God for taking her little girl."

The young woman continued to weep, holding our child tightly as Caressa continued to cling to her. Cherise and I were moved to tears As the crowd began to break up and return to their seats, many of them were staring at us, wondering what was going on.

I asked the young mother who was holding Caressa to listen to me. I said, "I'm a minister, and what I'm about to tell you is on video if you don't believe it. This past Saturday night, I had a dream. In the dream, God let me feel your grief. I saw my three-year-old in a coffin. I have never felt grief like that in my life. I went to church the next day and told my congregation about seeing my child in a coffin. The reason we're here today at SeaWorld is because my wife decided she wanted to come one day early. Now, I know why. God wanted you to know your precious daughter is with Him in heaven."

I went on to tell her that our three-year-old has never run into the arms of a complete stranger. "This is a sign from God to you of how much He loves you." I explained to her that King David, in the Bible, also lost a son and said, "*Can I bring him back again? I shall go to him, but he shall not return to me*" (2 Samuel 12:23). I told the woman, "You must determine, even though you can't bring back your child, that someday you will go to the place where your child has gone."

The whole family tearfully prayed with us. God's healing presence was so strong; we felt like we were standing on holy ground. While the young mother still held Caressa, our daughter began to play with a little pearl necklace around the mother's neck. The grieving mother had placed a similar necklace around the neck of her child as she lay in her casket. The woman unhooked the necklace and snapped it around Caressa's neck. In doing so, she was essentially letting go of her little girl and placing her in God's loving hands.

The young woman told us that this experience had restored her faith in God. After we all cried and prayed, it was time to go our separate ways. When we tried to pry Caressa from her arms, she threw a fit because she wanted to stay with the young woman. To us, that was stranger than anything else.

Suffering never leaves you where it finds you;
you either become bitter or better. It either turns you into a miserable
complainer, or conforms you into the image of Jesus Christ.

My wife and I will never forget that family standing and weeping as we walked away, with Caressa reaching back toward that mother. Think of the measures to which God will go just to tell us He loves us when we are hurting!

If we are hurting, He hurts, too. *"For we do not have a High Priest who cannot sympathize with our weaknesses"* (Hebrews 4:15). Jesus allowed himself to be forsaken by God so He could say, "I know, I've been there." Our God knows the pain of loss. He is moved by the same things that distress us.

Suffering never leaves you where it finds you; you either become bitter or better. It either turns you into a miserable complainer, or conforms you into the image of Jesus Christ. God loved that young mother so much that He gave me a dream, rearranged our schedule, gave my wife discernment to insist on leaving early, and He even used my three-year-old daughter's affections to move her to the right place at the right time—the arms of a broken, hurting woman.

Think of it. Out of thousands of people in that stadium, God put us in the right place, at the right time.

PROPER PLACEMENT

One of God's primary purposes for your life is proper placement. Being in the right place at the right time is an important key to discovering God's will for your life. In Genesis 1, God created Adam; in Genesis 2, God planted Adam into the proper place, a garden.

What does this tell you about God and His will for your life?

1.   God doesn't leave you where He finds you.

2.   God has a proper placement for you.

The owner of the first "placement service" in the world was God. Paul wrote, *"God has set the members, each one of them, in the body just as He pleased"* (1 Corinthians 12:18). God comes to you right where you are and gives you a purpose, a mission, and a place. God gave Adam a place of employment before He gave him a wife. If you're a single woman, you shouldn't consider marrying any man who doesn't have his place of employment—a job.

Proper placement profoundly affects your future in seven ways:

1.   It releases supernatural provision in your life.

2.   It provides protection.

3.   It demands the death of pride.

4.   It is often preceded by a season of discomfort.

5.   It releases the glory of God on your life.

6.   It prevents exposure to sinful situations and temptations you would encounter if improperly placed

7.   It can help you to avoid future problems

1. IT RELEASES SUPERNATURAL PROVISION

First Kings 17:3–4 describes supernatural provision:

Get away from here and turn eastward, and hide by the Brook Cherith, which flows into the Jordan. And it will be that you shall drink from the brook, and I have commanded the ravens to feed you there.

During a famine, God gave Elijah clear instruction saying, in effect, "Go to Cherith. I have commanded the ravens to feed you *there*." God told Elijah that if he moved to the right place, supernatural provision *will* show up. Divine supply follows divine placement. If Elijah had been any other place but the right place, the ravens would not have fed him. God holds your place of supernatural provision—God has a "there" for you!

Just about the time Elijah thought he had God all figured out, suddenly the brook dried up and the ravens stopped bringing food. I once preached a sermon called, "What to Do When the Brook Goes Dry and the Birds Won't Fly!" In it, I explained that the only reason God lets the brook dry up is because He wants to drive you back to your source. We are to seek God's face, not His hand. We want a handout, but God wants a face-off.

Don't fall in love with the method and forget that God is your source. The brook wasn't Elijah's source; God was. We get married to a method, anchored to a memory, but we must be open to change. When the Holy Spirit wants to do a new thing, we have to get away from the old wineskins. In this case, God gave Elijah a new plan, "Go to Zarephath…. I have commanded a widow there to provide for you" (1 Kings 17:9).

My wife has her own contracting company. She has such a great gift in this area that her talent has blessed us financially. In fact, the first home that we owned was one that she built. We lived with her parents for four years while saving all the money we could. Finally, we had enough money to buy an empty lake property that Cherise had found in Gainesville, Georgia. She really felt that we needed to stretch our resources and try to purchase it. We paid $50,000 for the lot, exhausting all the money we had. We secured a $130,000 loan for the home, and Cherise built a beautiful home on the lake. We lived in it for a year and then sold it for $389,000.

The story gets better. She later found another lot on the lake in a beautiful neighborhood. This lot was a whopping $180,000! That was almost the entire profit from the sale of our first home. I felt the lot was too costly and that we would never get our money out of it. Still, her amazing financial discernment caused her to persist. She said, "I can build a home on this lot and make a fortune." Thankfully, I listened to her. Today, the lot alone is valued at over one million dollars.

Through the years, my wife has had an uncanny ability to make wise financial investments in the area of real estate. Regretfully I have not always listened to her. Consequently, we've missed some incredible financial blessings. But I've learned that one of my wife's strong points is in business, so I'm glad to take a backseat to her in this area.

Discern the place of blessing for your life. If God says, "I'll bless you 'there,'" and you insist on staying "here," then you're going to miss His provision. Everything was dependent upon Elisha being in the right location.

When Ruth was looking for a place of provision, she expressed her desire to her mother-in-law, Naomi. *"Please let me go to the field, and glean heads of grain after him in whose sight I may find favor"* (Ruth 2:2). You don't want to work in just any field. Pray for discernment that will lead you into an occupational field where you will find the favor of your employer. The place God has for you will be a place of influence, favor, and prosperity.

Sometimes, the place God sends you won't appear to be a place of blessing. When Ruth found the right field in which to work, she labored in only a remote corner of it. Later, she was promoted from working in that insignificant corner to owning the entire field! But, her promotion was contingent upon finding the right place of employment.

Are you in the right place, or are you leaning on an old plow, afraid to let go?

In 2 Chronicles 7:12, God said, *"I have heard your prayer, and have chosen this place for Myself as a house of sacrifice."* Oh, the potential of a chosen place. If you are in such a place, don't leave it. If you are not, don't stay another day. In Exodus 33:21, God says, *"Here is a place by Me, and you shall stand on the rock."* There is a place reserved for you by God. If you will move there, God will supernaturally provide all you need to do His will.

2. IT PROVIDES A PLACE OF PROTECTION

A wrong place is any place where you know your Christian walk is compromised. When you stay out of the wrong places, you protect your integrity. Any place that Christ Himself would not go is the wrong environment. A good rule to follow is, "If Christ wouldn't, you shouldn't!"

In the cool of the day, Adam and Eve would walk with God in the garden of Eden. When they were together, Satan never showed up. He approached Eve when she was absent from God's presence.

As long as Peter stayed near Jesus' side, he was strong in faith; but when he was alone—absent from the presence of Jesus—he warmed his hands by the wrong fire and denied Christ three times. (See John 18:17–18, 25–27.)

There is protection in His presence. Don't stray too far from the body of Christ, which is the church, or you'll become easy prey for the enemy.

3. IT DEMANDS THE DEATH OF PRIDE

Proper placement demands the death of pride. This is a tough one! Pride is one of the main obstacles blocking your move to the right place. When we are puffed up with pride, we say things like, "Well, I'm not going to work there. I'm better than they are."

Elijah was a great and mighty man of God. He was a big, strong prophet who killed four hundred fifty prophets of Baal and called down fire from heaven. But in 1 Kings, God instructed him to seek help at the home of a widow, *"I have commanded a widow there to provide for you"* (1 Kings 17:9). This would have been a perfect time for pride to swell within Elijah. He could have said, "I'm not going to lower myself by asking for help from that woman." But he didn't allow pride to keep him from the right place.

Men can learn a lot from their wives, but pride won't let them say, "I was wrong, you were right." Often, finding your proper placement demands the death of personal pride.

4. IT IS OFTEN PRECEDED BY A SEASON OF DISCOMFORT

Proper placement is often preceded by a season of discomfort. The reason is simple: until your misery factor exceeds your fear factor, you won't change. We prize security.

When a mother eagle wants her eaglets to learn how to fly, she begins to tear up the nest. She removes the animal fur to expose the briars and thorns. Suddenly, the nest isn't such a comfortable place anymore, so the eaglets swiftly desire to stretch their wings and learn to soar. You'll never fly if you're too comfortable. You will never change that which you are willing to tolerate. God has a way of making us move out. It's called discomfort.

5. IT RELEASES THE GLORY OF GOD

Proper placement releases the glory of God on your life. In the book of Exodus, God told Moses how to construct the tabernacle:

> *I have put wisdom in the hearts of all who are gifted artisans, that they may make all that I have commanded you: the tabernacle of meeting, the ark of the Testimony and the mercy seat that is on it, and all the furniture of the tabernacle; the table and its utensils, the pure gold lampstand with all its utensils, the altar of incense, the altar of burnt offering with all its utensils, and the laver and its base; the garments of ministry, the holy garments for Aaron the priest and the garments of his sons, to minister as priests, and the anointing oil and sweet incense for the holy place. According to all that I have commanded you they shall do.* (Exodus 31:6–11)

God gave specific dimensions, colors, and furniture placement, even the garments that were to be worn there. They did exactly what God said, and the results were spectacular, *"Then the cloud covered the tabernacle of meeting, and the glory of the LORD filled the tabernacle"* (Exodus 40:34). In 2 Chronicles, after Solomon completed the more permanent temple and all the furniture was properly placed, the Scripture says, *"Fire came down from heaven and consumed the burnt offering and the sacrifices; and the glory of the LORD filled the temple"* (2 Chronicles 7:1). The right place, the right location, and the right job release the glory of God upon our lives.

6. IT PREVENTS EXPOSURE TO SINFUL SITUATIONS AND TEMPTATION

If you will listen to God's voice and get in the right place, God's glory will be your reward. Failing to do so may subject you to sinful situations and temptations.

The first words God spoke to Adam after he sinned referred to Adam's location, *"Then the LORD God called to Adam and said to him, 'Where are you?'"* (Genesis 3:9). Adam's sin drove him out of the place specifically prepared for him.

Lot was the nephew of Abram, but he left his uncle and moved to Sodom. What was he doing living in Sodom? Lot saw an opportunity to get rich, but eventually lost his wife in the process because he wasn't where he was supposed to be.

7. IT CAN HELP YOU TO AVOID FUTURE PROBLEMS

Living within the proper placement of God can make all the difference between a life of blessing and a life of sorrow. If you live in the right city, go to the right church, find the right job, hang out with the right people, and marry the right spouse, many potential problems will be averted.

How do you discover the right place? Repent, pray, and expect divine guidance.

REPENT: STOP DOING YOUR OWN THING

Psalm 92:13 says, "*Those who are planted in the house of the LORD shall flourish in the courts of our God.*" Don't be a tumbleweed Christian, fruitless and rootless, blowing in and out of churches. Get rooted and grounded in the right church.

The prodigal son finally came to his senses and realized that he was in the wrong place, living in a pigpen, when he said, "'*I will arise and go to my father*'" (Luke 15:18). He was saying, in effect, "I'm leaving the wrong place and going back to the right place." (See Luke 15:11–32.)

Don't be a tumbleweed Christian, fruitless and rootless,
blowing in and out of churches.
Get rooted and grounded in the right church.

PRAY FOR GOD'S TIMING AND GOD'S PLACE

We are not asking for something that God doesn't know. Acts 17:26 says, "*And He has made from one blood every nation of men to dwell on all the face of the earth, and has determined their preappointed times and the boundaries of their dwellings.*" According to Scripture, God assigns a place for you and sets a time for you to be there.

EXPECT DIVINE GUIDANCE

Missing God's will produces severe consequences. It is my belief that you are safer fighting in a war within the will of God than a day at the beach outside of the will of God.

It has been said, "If God closes one door, He will open another one." That is true, but you don't want to hang out very long in the hallway. When God closes one door and you're standing in the hallway waiting for the next door to open, yearn, hunger for His divine guidance. "*The steps of a good man are ordered by the LORD*" (Psalm 37:23).

The voice of discernment God has placed within you will lead you to the right places where you will make Kingdom Connections (the right people, at the right place, at the right time). Learn to listen to your inner voice of discernment in order to release supernatural provision into your life and the lives of those you meet.

God has a SeaWorld assignment for you. Someone out there is in his or her dark night of the soul. They are counting on you to be sensitive enough to God's leading that you will be in the right place at the right time so He can use you to shine His light into their darkness.

Take a moment now to stop and reflect on what you have read, and what it means to you and for your life. Consider each of the questions below and journal your answers. Date this page, so that when you look back, you will have a record of your journey in this season of life. Any time the Lord speaks to you, it is important to record it.

DATE: _____

CHAPTER 6 QUESTIONS:

1. Give a brief summary of your readings for chapter 6.

_____

_____

_____

_____

2. List two key points that were discussed in chapter 6, then give your understanding of each of those key points.

_____

_____

_____

_____

3. Chapter 6 talks about being in the "right place," but it also says the "right" place is preceded by a place of discomfort. Write about the place where you are right now as it relates to the two talked about in chapter 6.

_____

_____

_____

_____

Please do not rush through the following set of insights into your purpose. Make sure you are someplace where you won't be interrupted for the next ten minutes. Following are some very important questions that I would like you to consider and write responses to. When you have cleared your mind and opened your heart, take a moment to consider and journal about the experience.

Close your eyes and imagine for a moment your ideal place of work or your ideal place of purpose. Just take a minute to let that place fill in around you as it becomes clearer in your mind's eye.

Questions:

1. What kinds of things are you doing there?

_____

_____

_____

2. Who is there with you?

_____

_____

_____

3. Who are you serving in that place?

_____

_____

_____

4. Does that place have a name?

_____

_____

_____

5. Who do you know that is currently doing what you are doing in that place?

_____

_____

_____

_____

CHAPTER 6 CONCLUDING REFLECTION

Your reflection should include the following:

+ What you learned

+ What had the most value for you or had direct application to your life

+ Any other takeaways

_____

_____

_____

_____

_____

_____

_____

_____

_____

_____

_____

_____

_____

_____

_____

_____

_____

_____

_____

_____

7

RIGHT PLAN

> *For I know the thoughts that I think toward you,*
> *says the LORD, thoughts of peace and not of evil,*
> *to give you a future and a hope.*
> —Jeremiah 29:11

There is a right plan. One idea from God can change your life. Thomas Edison had one idea, and today we have the electric light bulb. The Wright brothers had one idea, and now we have aviation. Bill Gates had one idea, and today we have the personal computer. There are "good ideas," and there are "God ideas." The Holy Spirit wants you to discern the difference between the two.

PRAY FOR A MIRACLE—GET A PLAN

Perhaps, today, you need a miracle, for you or for your family. When you ask God for a miracle, He will often give you a set of instructions—a plan. He rarely releases a miracle without a plan. Too often we pray and then sit back and wait for God to do miracles. If you read your Bible, however, you'll find it doesn't work that way. You want a miracle? You're going to receive a set of instructions—a plan.

When Joshua needed a miracle of conquest, God gave him a plan.

You shall march around the city, all you men of war; you shall go all around the city once. This you shall do six days. And seven priests shall bear seven trumpets of rams' horns before the ark. But the seventh day you shall march around the city seven times, and the priests shall blow the trumpets. It shall come to pass, when they make a long blast with the ram's horn, and when you hear the sound of the trumpet, that all the people shall shout with a great

shout; then the wall of the city will fall down flat. And the people shall go up
every man straight before him   (Joshua 6:3–5)

God said, in effect, "Here's the plan: march seven times and on the seventh day, march seven times. Then blow the horns and shout—and the walls will fall." Joshua obeyed, and God's plan brought the walls of Jericho down.

When Naaman sought a miracle of healing for his leprosy, God provided a plan through the prophet Elisha. *"Go and wash in the Jordan seven times, and your flesh shall be restored to you, and you shall be clean"* (2 Kings 5:10). That simple set of instructions from God brought a miraculous healing to Naaman's body. (See verse 14.)

Before Samson was born, God appeared to his mother and said, *"For behold, you shall conceive and bear a son. And no razor shall come upon his head, for the child shall be a Nazarite to God from the womb; and he shall begin to deliver Israel out of the hand of the Philistines"* (Judges 13:5). God already had a detailed plan for his life before the boy was even born.

Similar stories are told in the New Testament. In the first chapter of Luke, Elizabeth and Zacharias were told by the angel of God they would have a son. Very little was left to chance.

Your wife Elizabeth will bear you a son, and you shall call his name John. And you will have joy and gladness, and many will rejoice at his birth. For he will be great in the sight of the Lord, and shall drink neither wine nor strong drink. He will also be filled with the Holy Spirit, even from his mother's womb. And he will turn many of the children of Israel to the Lord their God. He will also go before Him in the spirit and power of Elijah, "to turn the hearts of the fathers to the children," and the disobedient to the wisdom of the just, to make ready a people prepared for the Lord.

(Luke 1:13–17)

Once again, the plan of God came, his name and assignment, before Elizabeth was even pregnant with John the Baptist, their miracle child.

At the wedding in Cana, when Mary asked her son for a miracle of provision, Jesus gave her a plan. Mary had enough experience with the plans of God that she knew what to do.

His mother said to the servants, "Whatever He says to you, do it." Now there were set there six waterpots of stone, according to the manner of purification of the Jews, containing twenty or thirty gallons apiece. Jesus said to them, "Fill the waterpots with water." And they filled them up to the brim.

And He said to them, "Draw some out now, and take it to the master of the feast." And they took it. (John 2:5–8)

The water blushed in the presence of its Creator, turning into wine of the highest caliber. (See John 2:9–10.) When you ask God for a miracle, He connects your miracle result to a miracle plan.

KNOW THE SOURCE

Jeremiah 29:11 says, *"For I know the thoughts that I think toward you, says the* LORD, *thoughts of peace and not of evil, to give you a future and a hope."* God made you for a purpose. When you don't know why something is made, you can easily abuse it. Don't ask the creation what its purpose is; ask its Creator.

Some of you may be thinking, *You don't know where I came from, the things I've done. You don't know my parents. I came from an illegitimate background.*

That doesn't matter to God.

Here's what you need to understand: *"Before I formed you in the womb I knew you; before you were born I sanctified you; I ordained you a prophet to the nations"* (Jeremiah 1:5). You don't come from a background. You don't come from your parents. You may have come *through* them, but you didn't come *from* them. You come from God. Your assignment can't be messed up by your circumstances.

Ephesians 2:10 reminds us, *"For we are His workmanship, created in Christ Jesus for good works, which God prepared beforehand that we should walk in them."* When you were created, God encoded you for an assignment, and He gave you the power to get it done. The enemy's job is to pull us out of that divine assignment, out of the will of God.

You don't come from a background. You don't come from your parents. You may have come through *them, but you didn't come* from *them. You come from God.*

Every assignment has a birthplace. Destiny is reached by discerning those transitional moments when God sends you His roadmap leading to your purpose.

The church I pastor, Free Chapel, has been in existence for over sixty years. When I was a full-time evangelist, the former pastor, Roy Wellborn, would schedule me to come preach a revival every year. The last time I preached for Pastor Wellborn, it was scheduled nine months in advance. Just prior to the date, however, he became ill, was hospitalized, and passed away. He died on Friday night; I was to preach that Sunday.

The congregation loved Pastor Wellborn. They were devastated by his passing. You can imagine how inadequate I felt standing in the pulpit two days after his death—the pulpit this beloved man had faithfully filled for over thirty years. As soon as the morning's service ended, they rolled the coffin in and held Pastor Wellborn's memorial service.

At that time, I had no idea that I was there by the divine plan of almighty God. I'm sure that when Pastor Wellborn scheduled me to preach in his church, he had no idea he would be in heaven that very week, or that God had already chosen me as his replacement.

God really does have a marvelous plan for our lives. Pray for special insight into His plans for your life. You will discover that "*eye has not seen, nor ear heard, nor have entered into the heart of man the things which God has prepared for those who love Him*" (1 Corinthians 2:9).

GOD'S UNEXPECTED PLAN

God's plan for your life will often come through unexpected events that force you in a direction you never would have gone. Esther experienced the providential leading of God that gave her assignment a "birthplace."

The book of Esther opens with a wild seven-day party in the king's palace. King Ahasuerus asked all of his council of warlords to join him on his next military expedition. He was hungry for power. In order to sell his idea, he decided to "wine and dine" his warlords for seven days.

At the end of seven days of partying, the epitome of the seduction was flaunting the best-looking women in the king's harem in dance. These shapely, beautiful women danced before the drunken warlords, ensuring that they would be ready to follow the king into battle wherever he led them.

As the icing on the cake, the custom was to bring the queen out to dance in order to close the deal. There was nothing unusual about the king asking Queen Vashti to dance; what was unusual was for her to refuse. When the queen failed to appear, one of his warlords exclaimed,

The queen's behavior will become known to all women, so that they will despise their husbands in their eyes, when they report, "King Ahasuerus commanded Queen Vashti to be brought in before him, but she did not come." This very day the noble ladies of Persia and Media will say to all the

king's officials that they have heard of the behavior of the queen. Thus there
will be excessive contempt and wrath.   (Esther 1:17–18)

Greatly embarrassed, King Ahasuerus decided to get rid of his queen. Suddenly, here was a king without a queen. In order to find a new queen, the palace announced a national beauty contest. One hundred twenty-seven women were selected from the provinces for the king's consideration. Esther, a young orphan girl, was chosen as one of them.

Queen Vashti's fatal attitude set the stage for the higher purpose of God. Sometimes, when things happen you can't explain, these paradoxical occurrences tell us somebody else is in charge. As Christians, we don't believe things happen by chance; instead, we believe God has a plan for our lives. It's interesting how God often seems to use people with disadvantaged backgrounds—Esther was an orphan. God has a habit of picking up *nobodies* and making them into *somebodies.*

Overnight, God placed the orphaned girl, Esther, in the palace. Her godly uncle, Mordecai, had raised her and groomed her for greatness. She knew she was special, even if she didn't have pretty shoes and lived in a little hut. Mordecai had taught her about her covenant relationship with God.

Many times, like Esther, we are oblivious to God's plan for our lives. Esther was looking for an ordinary life. She probably dreamed of raising a traditional Jewish family, leading a typical existence, not knowing she was meant for extraordinary things. I'm sure she dreamed of holding hands with her fiancé under the olive tree and planning her wedding ceremony. But while she was planning everyday things, God was planning supernatural opportunities for her.

While we are so busy grabbing lesser things, ordinary things,
mediocre things, God is planning extraordinary things for our future.
Don't let anyone tell you that you can't reach for the stars.

In the same way, when we are so busy grabbing lesser things, ordinary things, mediocre things, God is planning extraordinary things for our future. Don't let anyone tell you that you can't reach for the stars. Even if you don't get there today, you possess the possibility that, maybe tomorrow, you will make it. *"We know that all things work together for good to those who love God, to those who are the called according to His purpose"* (Romans 8:28).

A godly man laid the groundwork in Esther's childhood to prepare her for her life assignment. Esther had been groomed, psychologically and spiritually, to become great. When the king selected his new queen, out of all those women, he chose Esther.

God always sets a mentor alongside to give insight, wisdom, and direction. Esther had her Mordecai, Ruth had her Naomi, and Mary had her Elizabeth. Timothy had the faith of his mother and grandmother, *"When I call to remembrance the genuine faith that is in you, which dwelt first in your grandmother Lois and your mother Eunice, and I am persuaded is in you also"* (2 Timothy 1:5).

You could be your children's mentor. What you speak into your children's lives today may prepare them for unexpected greatness and unlimited opportunities.

God had a higher purpose for young Esther than being the king's contest winner. Before this young girl was selected from her province to enter the contest, she didn't know proper protocol; she hadn't been taught formal table manners; she didn't know how to curtsy; she didn't know the right clothes to wear; she didn't display manners befitting royalty. Yet God selected this ignorant orphan girl, fresh from the hills. Like Cinderella, her foot fit the glass slipper and she found favor with the king.

The king chose Esther, not because she was Jewish or because he had a spiritual revelation. He was simply using his senses, unaware that God was guiding his eyes.

Did you know that God is able to use people who aren't spiritual? Have you ever had someone say to you, "I don't know why I'm doing this for you; I don't know why I'm breaking the rules for you"? They're telling the truth—they don't know why they're helping you. They can't intelligently explain why they want to help you. When you're in God's will, He'll even use your enemies to make a way for you. Proverbs 16:7 says, *"When a man's ways please the LORD, He makes even his enemies to be at peace with him."*

THE PROCESS

Once Esther was in the palace, she had to go through a purification process. Along with the call of God comes "the process." We like to be called out and chosen by God, but for every calling there is a discipline.

OIL

First, Esther had to soak in oil for six months. In Scripture, oil signifies the Holy Spirit. I'm sure her feet were calloused from walking barefoot in the hills and mountains. She had to be oiled down in order to smooth the skin between her toes and on the soles of her feet. Before God can use you, He has to soak you in the Holy Spirit to take away the rough places in your life.

This woman was going to determine the fate of her nation. She had to be anointed. She was affecting future generations. Queen Vashti was an independent woman concerned with doing her own thing, but Esther understood it was not about her thing; it was about following God's plan.

By soaking in oil every day for six months, Esther represented a woman of God becoming extremely attuned to the Holy Spirit. Women, don't think you're a freak because you're spiritually sensitive. You're not a person who has only a mind and a body, but you also have a spirit. Therefore, you're spiritual, not just cute. You can wear a beautiful dress and makeup, but still have Holy Spirit anointing underneath. Don't be ashamed of your spirituality.

Men, sometimes your friends will make fun of you for being spiritually minded. They may mock your sensitivity and compassion while tempting you to revert back to your cold, detached, self-reliant past. Ask yourself, *How is that working out for my so-called "friend?"* Remember that it takes more courage and machismo to remain sensitive to the things of God than it does to run from Him and live life on your own.

Praise is more than making a noise. When you praise Him, you invite the presence of God, the calm of God, and the serenity of God into your life.

PERFUME

The second step of Esther's purification process was being perfumed. You know what perfume does. It makes you smell nice; it draws people to you. In the Bible, incense represents our praise to God. There was an altar of incense in the Old Testament tabernacle. When the priest poured the perfume on the hot coals of the altar of incense, the scent would go up to heaven. The Bible says that God received the incense offering as a sweet-smelling savor of praise. (See Leviticus 2:2.) Of course, under the new covenant, we don't have to sprinkle incense on a fire. All we have to do is open up our mouths and give God the fruit of our lips, which is the fragrance of praise in His nostrils. (See Hebrews 13:15.)

When we praise God verbally, it's like spraying the most expensive perfume or cologne; it goes up to heaven and creates an aroma that gets God's attention. Praise is more than making a noise. When you praise Him, you invite the presence of God, the calm of God, and the serenity of God into your life.

Praise is called "the oil of myrrh." Remember the wise men who came to Bethlehem when Jesus was born? They brought frankincense and myrrh, which denote praise and adoration. Learn to be a worshipper.

Esther's scent reached the king before she did. The reason the king extended his scepter to Esther was that she filled the throne room with her perfume of praise before she was given access into the king's presence. We, too, come into God's presence first by the aroma of our praise.

No wonder the ultimate worshipper, the psalmist David, said, *"Enter into His gates with thanksgiving, and into His courts with praise. Be thankful to Him, and bless His name"* (Psalm 100:4). Esther was chosen, groomed, oiled, and perfumed.

When you praise, you get a sense of what God wants you to do. With praise comes prophecy. With praise comes direction. With praise comes God's plan for your life.

I'm sure that after six months of bubble baths, massages, pedicures, manicures, pampering, the opulence of the palace, and the luxurious lifestyle Esther was afforded, she began to dull a little spiritually. If you are not careful, you may become so pampered and comfortable spiritually that you will forget there is a godly reason for being where you are. This is no time to get comfortable! There is still a plot to annihilate our children, our homes, our marriages, and our nation. You have a call of God upon your life; you have an appointment with destiny.

While Esther got comfortable and almost forgot her purpose, Mordecai put on sackcloth. (See Esther 4:1.) Sackcloth is ugly-looking clothing. He got ugly. Every now and then, we have to "get ugly" to get God's attention. We have to afflict ourselves with fasting and prayer.

Mordecai reminded Esther that she was not just there to look good and to wear beautiful clothing. No, there was a mission!

> *Do not think in your heart that you will escape in the king's palace any more than all the other Jews. For if you remain completely silent at this time, relief and deliverance will arise for the Jews from another place, but you and your father's house will perish. Yet who knows whether you have come to the kingdom for such a time as this?* (Esther 4:13–14)

Don't forget your purpose. To all of you Esthers out there, there is a plot to destroy your family. We all enjoy being pampered, but there is a battle to fight and a victory to win. There is a cause!

Esther got the message from Mordecai, and she sent word back, saying in effect, "I was a little foggy for a while. I went on a fantasy trip, but now I'm back on course. I've made a decision about my purpose. I know what God has called me to do, and I've got to make this move." Esther said, *"And if I perish, I perish!"* (verse 16). The result was that Esther preserved her race.

"Who knows whether you have come to the kingdom for such a time as this?" It is time for you to make your move. Up until now you've been merely looking the part. Gentlemen, you hang in the back all cool and detached. Ladies, you sit in church like a fashion model. Now, your time is up. Maybe two years ago you could afford to play God-games, but now it's your time. Don't forget your purpose. Move out and do it—submit to God's will. Be anointed with the oil of the Holy Spirit; be perfumed with passionate praise for God. You have come to the kingdom for such a time as this. Jesus prayed, *"Not My will, but Yours, be done"* (Luke 22:42). Pray and expect God to give you the right plan for your life.

Stay open to divine interruptions; when God does a new thing it's not like the old thing. Lot's wife only appears one time in Scripture. Why did Jesus tell us to remember her? (See Luke 17:32.) It was because she refused to break up with her past. She turned into a lifeless monument. Stop rehearsing your beginning, and write the rest of your story. In Isaiah, God even told His prophet, *"Behold, I will do a new thing, now it shall spring forth"* (Isaiah 43:19). If you're afraid of the future, check your past. He has never failed you.

Take a moment now to stop and reflect on what you have read, and what it means to you and for your life. Consider each of the questions below and journal your answers. Date this page, so that when you look back, you will have a record of your journey in this season of life. Any time the Lord speaks to you, it is important to record it.

DATE: _____

CHAPTER 7 QUESTIONS:

1. Give a brief summary of your readings for chapter 7.

_____

_____

_____

_____

2. List three to five key points that were discussed and then give your understanding for each of those key points.

_____

_____

_____

_____

3. Think about the questions from chapter 6:

- What is your ideal place of work or your place of purpose?
- What kinds of things are you doing there?
- Who is there with you?
- Who are you serving in that place?
- Does that place have a name?
- Who do you know that is currently doing what you are doing in that place?

As you think about those questions, tell me three things you can do right now, that will start you moving in that direction.

_____

_____

_____

_____

4. What obstacles stand between you and moving more fully in the direction of that divine plan?

_____

_____

_____

_____

5. When you look at the seasons of your life over the years, do you see a pattern or a plan that emerges or any central themes that come forward? If so, what are they?

_____

_____

_____

6. Based on what you have learned in this chapter, are there any areas of your life in which you will begin to act or think differently?

_____

_____

_____

_____

CHAPTER 7 CONCLUDING REFLECTION

Your reflection should include the following:

+ What you learned

+ What had the most value for you or had direct application to your life

+ Any other takeaways

_____

_____

_____

_____

_____

_____

_____

_____

_____

_____

_____

_____

_____

_____

_____

_____

_____

_____

_____

_____

PART III

UNLOCKING DISCERNMENT

8

WAIT ON THE LORD

Whoever believes will not act hastily.
—Isaiah 28:16

For a time in 2005, I was ashamed to tell anybody where I was from. Every time I turned on the news, all I saw and heard was "the Runaway Bride from Gainesville, Georgia." It was constant. My heart went out to those families, and to the bride herself, that such a personal and traumatic moment would suddenly become such public fodder.

The truth is, there are scores of bad marriages in this world because the people rushed into them. There was pressure or fear or emotion, and they just went ahead with it. People had told the Gainesville couple, "You need to wait." Counselors told them, "You need to wait." People they respected spiritually told them, "You need to wait." Let me weigh in with my two cents: if you are confused about whether or not you want to marry someone to the point that you're ready to run away, you don't need to marry that person—ever!

In 1 Samuel 13, we read about a man who had trouble waiting. Saul was the king of the nation of Israel, which was being besieged by the Philistine army. The prophet Samuel told Saul that war was indeed coming. Through Samuel, God instructed Saul to go to the temple and wait for seven days. After that, Samuel would come and offer a sacrifice, and God would then go with them into battle. Simple enough, right? Wrong.

Scripture says,

Then he waited seven days, according to the time set by Samuel. But Samuel did not come to Gilgal; and the people were scattered from him. So Saul said, "Bring a burnt offering and peace offerings here to me." And he offered the burnt offering.

(1 Samuel 13:8–9)

Soon after that, Samuel arrived and Saul went out to greet him. Samuel asked what Saul had done. Saul replied,

When I saw that the people were scattered from me, and that you did not come within the days appointed, and that the Philistines gathered together at Michmash, then I said, "The Philistines will now come down on me at Gilgal, and I have not made supplication to the LORD." Therefore I felt compelled, and offered a burnt offering. (verses 11–12)

Do you hear what Saul was saying? "The people were expecting me to do something. You weren't here. Nothing was happening. I wasn't just going to sit there. I had to something. The people expected me to do something."

Samuel's response was,

You have done foolishly. You have not kept the commandment of the LORD your God, which He commanded you. For now the LORD would have established your kingdom over Israel forever. But now your kingdom shall not continue. The LORD has sought for Himself a man after His own heart, and the LORD has commanded him to be commander over His people, because you have not kept what the LORD commanded you.

(1 Samuel 13:13–14)

Do you see what's going on here? If Saul had simply waited as he was instructed, there would have never been a need for David. The Lord would have established His kingdom with Saul.

God has a perfect time and a correct way for everything. We can get ourselves into trouble when we don't train ourselves to wait on Him. *"Whoever believes will not act hastily"* (Isaiah 28:16). If you believe that God only wants what is best for your life, and you are following Him, then He is ultimately in control of your life—your family, your career, your finances, your decisions, everything!

In other words, don't rush into things! Don't do things because people are putting pressure on you. People can mess their lives up when they jump into things even though, in their hearts, they're hearing, *Hold on* and *Wait.*

"Whoever believes will not act hastily." Whoever believes will not quickly jump into anything.

But those who wait on the LORD shall renew their strength; they shall mount up with wings like eagles. (Isaiah 40:31)

Wait on the LORD; *be of good courage, and He shall strengthen your heart;*
wait, I say, on the LORD! (Psalm 27:14)

WAITING FINANCIALLY

People today just have to have it all right now. Years ago, buying something on credit was actually considered a bad thing. It's what people with no money did. Now, people would never consider saving money for a big purchase. Why wait when you can have it now?

I've heard people say, "Well, I don't really feel a peace about that house, but we walked through it and we just felt chill bumps. It's the house we've always wanted." But, can you afford that house? Can you make the payment every month?

Maybe now is not the right time. Does that mean that you can never have it? No, but it might mean that now is not the right time. It means, *"Whoever believes will not act hastily."*

People make stupid decisions trying to keep up with the Joneses, only to find out, when they catch up with the Joneses, that they are up to their eyeballs in debt. People make stupid financial decisions because they don't use discernment; they don't wait on the Lord. Wait and save your money. Be patient. Don't try to get everything now. Wait!

DON'T FORCE IT

God's timing is perfect. If you're being pressured, that's the time when you need to pull back. You need to pray and fast. You need to go to the Word. Then, after you've prayed with your spouse, fasted, and gone to the Word, you need to talk to some of your Christian friends, or perhaps a pastor, and say, "Help me pray about this." *"By the mouth of two or three witnesses"* (2 Corinthians 13:1) every major decision of your life ought to be confirmed. It should not just be you. You don't just walk through any opened door.

God does not push; God leads. God does not force; God leads.

God does not push; God leads. God does not force; God leads. Don't jeopardize God's best by becoming impatient trying to make something happen in your life that only He can release. I think about how many men of God I've known who bit the dust because they became impatient. That they began to think, *The rules don't apply to me anymore. I can take things into my own hands.* They climbed to incredible heights, reaching masses of people, but somewhere they lost touch with reality and raced ahead of God.

That is what happened to Saul. You have to be careful when God blesses you. You can get to the place where you believe that the rules, God's Word, don't apply to you anymore. Years earlier, God had spoken to Saul through the prophet Samuel, saying, "Saul, don't offer the sacrifice." But Saul's fear overcame his faith in God's Word, and he took matters into his own hands.

I don't care how much money you have. I don't care how much power you have. I don't care how much influence you have. I don't care what success you have. If you don't use discernment, if you don't wait on the Lord, it's only a matter of time before it catches up with you! You will become self-indulgent and lose your spiritual sensitivity. That's what happened to Saul.

If you are in the business world, you need to understand this. When God blesses you with prestige and position and power, you need spiritual discernment to know when you start to drift away and think the rules don't apply anymore. You need to continue to wait on the Lord and not resort to illegal or immoral shortcuts that fatten up the bottom line.

FACING YOUR GOLIATH

Here's why this is so important. While Saul was caught up in his own thing—offering his own sacrifices, not listening to anybody, not waiting on God—Goliath was on his way. Saul had never encountered Goliath before, but God knew Goliath was coming. Two chapters later, Goliath arrived to find Saul trembling in his tent. Why? When you begin to do your own thing, when you don't wait on the Lord or seek His counsel, Goliath shows up and you have no confidence—no courage. Saul was not ready to fight Goliath. Scripture says that by merely *"hearing the Philistine's words, Saul and all the Israelites were dismayed and terrified"* (1 Samuel 17:11). He was afraid because he hadn't learned to wait on the Lord. Fortunately, there was a boy named David who knew how to wait on the Lord, worship the Lord, and praise the Lord, so that, when Goliath came, he wasn't afraid.

I'm simply telling you this: Goliath is coming. You can't afford to disconnect from God. You can't afford to just ignore the convictions of the Holy Spirit and not wait on the Lord. Spend time with Him. Seek His face. Make no mistake, Goliath is coming. You say, "Oh, I've already faced it. Ooh. Let me tell my testimony." I promise you, another one will come! They come in seasons—the Goliath of something wrong with one of your children, the financial Goliath, the career Goliath, the health Goliath. I don't know what your Goliath will be, but I know it's coming and you don't want to be trembling in your tent when it does. You don't want to be cold and indifferent. You don't want to be ignoring everything God's told you to do when your Goliath comes.

Scripture states that Goliath was an overpowering figure, *"a man of war from his youth"* (1 Samuel 17:33). That means that many men had tried to defeat him in battle, but none ever had. When crisis comes, a fear will come in your heart. But if you are really in touch with God, something greater rises up inside of you and says, "I will not panic. I will not dread. I will not fear. God is with me. He's on the throne. It's going to be all right."

There are people reading this book who are going too fast and furious. They're trying to make something fit that doesn't fit. You're trying to force it to fit. Finally, you do kind of get it to fit, but now there's another piece that won't fit. It just messes the whole puzzle up. That's just like your life! If it doesn't fit, don't force it! If it doesn't feel right, wait on the Lord because *"whoever believes will not act hastily."*

Waiting on the Lord means that you will recognize His will and His voice. That doesn't mean that you become paralyzed by analyzing everything to death. It doesn't mean that you are waiting for an angel to appear, or putting out some kind of fleece.

Rest in the fact that God knows how to speak to His children and that *"by the mouth of two or three witnesses every word shall be established"* (2 Corinthians 13:1). Wait on Him and those witnesses will come forth. Even if it's a good opportunity, make sure it's a God opportunity!

Take a moment now to stop and reflect on what you have read, and what it means to you and for your life. Consider each of the questions below and journal your answers. Date this page, so that when you look back, you will have a record of your journey in this season of life. Any time the Lord speaks to you, it is important to record it.

DATE: _____

CHAPTER 8 QUESTIONS:

1. List two key points that were discussed and give your understanding for each of those key points.

_____

_____

_____

_____

2. Based on what you have read so far, explain your understanding of what it means to "wait on the Lord."

_____

_____

_____

_____

3. Chapter 8 talks about "facing your Goliath." Who or what, would you say, is your Goliath?

_____

_____

_____

_____

4. What is it out there that intimidates you or seems unconquerable? What do you do with it?

_____

_____

_____

_____

5. When you look at the season of your life over the years, do you see a pattern of Goliaths in your past? Is there anything in common about those Goliaths?

_____

_____

_____

_____

6. Based on what you have learned in this chapter, are there any areas of your life in which you will begin to act or think differently?

_____

_____

_____

_____

CHAPTER 8 CONCLUDING REFLECTION

Your reflection should include the following:

+ What you learned

+ What had the most value for you or had direct application to your life

+ Any other takeaways

_____

_____

_____

_____

_____

_____

_____

_____

_____

_____

_____

_____

_____

_____

_____

_____

_____

9

GUARDING THE UNGUARDED MOMENTS

*Blessed is the L*ORD *God of Israel, who sent you this day to meet me! And*
blessed is your advice and blessed are you, because you have kept me this day
from coming to bloodshed and from avenging myself with my own hand.
—1 Samuel 25:32–33

Sometimes I am reminded of what a typical Sunday morning in the Franklin home used to be. I would be up and out at 5:00 a.m., putting the finishing touches on my sermon. Back at the house, Cherise was left to deal with getting five kids dressed and ready for church. Have you ever tried to get five kids ready for church by yourself, plus get yourself ready? Sometimes she felt like she was in a trial run for the battle of Armageddon!

One Sunday morning, I received a frantic phone call. "I've had it," she said, "I can't take it anymore. I've reached my breaking point." After she had all the kids fully dressed, Drake, our seven-year-old at the time, spilled something all over his clothes. Connar, only a year older, could not find her shoes anywhere. Courteney and Caressa, who were teenagers, were fighting over who got to wear what blouse. Caroline, who was twelve at the time, ate too much candy the night before and was feeling sick. There's nothing like the joy of getting ready to be in the house of the Lord! By the time Cherise arrived at church, twenty minutes late, she was so frazzled she wished she had pulled the sheets over her head and stayed in bed!

THE "UNGUARDED MOMENT"

Have you ever been there? If so, you know how David felt when he had what I call an "unguarded moment."

David was anointed king during Saul's reign over Israel. But he did not go to the throne immediately. He was anointed at seventeen, but he was not appointed until he was about thirty.

As David's thirtieth birthday approached, the clock was ticking and none of God's promises had come into fruition in his life. How can God say one thing, but the circumstances of your life say otherwise? Often, before you reach your dream, you will experience the opposite of what you want. Abraham was dreaming for Isaac, the promised child; but first he experienced Ishmael, the problem child. The children of Israel were dreaming for a land flowing with milk and honey, but first they experienced the desert with no food or water. Jacob dreamed of a beautiful bride named Rachel, but first he was tricked into marrying Leah.

To make matters worse, David was leading six hundred men who were in debt, under distress, and feeling discontentment. David rose to the task of training them into a mighty army.

One day, they approached the vineyard of a man named Nabal, a rich man married to a very beautiful and intelligent woman named Abigail. Although Nabal acted foolishly, Abigail used her discernment to honor David, the man of God. (See 1 Samuel 25:2–42.) David's men decided to protect and guard Nabal's vineyard, and instead of asking for payment in money, they asked for food to replenish their strength. Nabal acted just like his name, which means "foolish." He refused to give them any food, and then, adding insult to injury, he accused David of being a servant who had broken away from his master. In other words, he called David a "nobody." Nabal insulted David by refusing him.

In order to appreciate David's reaction, you need to understand the crucial point at which David was living at that moment. David represents men who are in a transition in their lives; men who are close to reaching their dreams, yet whose fulfillment seems so far away. They're living on an unrealized promise! David had to be wondering, *Did God really say that I would reign as king, or was I just fantasizing?*

For thirteen years, David had been hanging onto that promise. He had believed God every step of the way, but now he had come to his breaking point. At this tender, touchy moment, along came Nabal. In the midst of David's spiritually frustration, what God had said about his future was not foremost in his mind. All he could think about at that moment was his location and his hunger.

In this unguarded moment, David assembled four hundred of his fiercest warriors and said, *"Every man gird on his sword"* (1 Samuel 25:13). And they set out to kill Nabal and his entire family.

Nabal was about to feel David's wrath. With his promised goals and throne eluding him, David lost it. How many of us can relate to this? Endless loads of thankless laundry, screaming children, unsympathetic bosses, then somebody cuts you off in traffic and you just want to scream, "I can't take it anymore!" You've reached the breaking point! You're having an unguarded moment.

You never know when it's going to happen. Human emotion is unpredictable. And Christians are certainly not exempt from those times when life's pressure brings out our rawest, deepest emotions. Yet, all it takes is that one unguarded moment and you can lose your reputation, your testimony, and even your ministry.

One Wednesday night years ago, I experienced an unguarded moment. I was taking the children home from our Wednesday night service. Cherise had gone out of town, and I had all five of the children by myself. I finally had them all hooked into their car seats and started on our way home when they informed me that they were starving.

We stopped at a fast-food restaurant down the road that has big yellow arches! The Wednesday night prior, we had stopped at the same restaurant and gone through the drive-thru window where I specifically asked for five cheeseburger kids' meals with no onions and no pickles. We drove all the way home, and, when the children opened up their food, onions were all over the place. They all threw fits and went to bed hungry, and I felt frustrated.

So, here we were again the following Wednesday night, same restaurant, same drive-thru, same lady at the window. I rolled down my window and began to speak to the little box. I was extremely nice, of course, because I'm Pastor Franklin—and because some of my members were in the line behind me!

I pleaded with the little box, "Please, ma'am, no onions. This is extremely important: no onions and no pickles. We asked for this last week, and you didn't do it. Please take care of it this week. Make sure our cheeseburgers have no onions and no pickles."

She said, "I'll handle it."

We pulled on through and were handed our five meals. The kids asked, "Can we eat it in the car, Dad?" "Absolutely not," I responded, "you are going to eat it at home. I'm not going to have that mess in my car for another month!"

We made it home, and I walked in the door with two or three of the kids screaming like they were starving to death. I opened up cheeseburger number one and looked at it—no onions, and no pickles...and no meat! There was only a slice of cheese with a blob of ketchup and mustard! I took cheeseburger number two, ditto! I looked at cheeseburger number three, same thing! By now, steam was whistling out of my ears and my eyes were rolling around in my head like the child in *The Exorcist*. I was ready to tell somebody what they could do with those cheeseburgers!

I called the restaurant and demanded, "I want a manager! Who owns this restaurant? I want a name and a phone number!" The girls were very supportive, saying, "Get'em, Daddy! Get'em, Daddy! You tell'em, Daddy!" About halfway through, it dawned on me that I had just stood in the pulpit that evening, and now I was about to let somebody have it. Perhaps I wasn't going to kill somebody, like David, but wasn't it Jesus who said, "*You have heard that it was said…'Do not murder, and anyone who murders will be subject to judgment.' But I tell you that anyone who is angry with his brother will be subject to judgment*" (Matthew 5:21–22 NIV)? Oops.

In David's life, at the point when he was about to kill Nabal, God sent a woman of great discernment into his life. It's always good to have discerning people around you. Abigail's wisdom had nothing to do with her beauty, her education, or the fact that she was married to a wealthy man. She had discernment because she feared the Lord, and she could think fast to defuse an explosive situation in her home. She believed what God had said about David—that he truly would become king—so she stood firmly on the Word of God to save her family. In this critical, transitional time in David's life, he needed to run into an Abigail.

It's always good for us to meet an Abigail, but especially when we're in transition. When we're trying to build a small business, but can't get the loan. When we're counting on getting a raise, but it hasn't come through yet. When we're searching for a job, but haven't found one. When we have to relocate, but can't sell the old house. When we're chasing our dream, but can't quite reach the top. These are dangerous, tricky times; times when we need an Abigail to cross our path.

When Abigail heard that David was coming to destroy her family, she did not crumble in the face of impending crisis. Instead, she prepared baskets of food. She knew in God's Word, "*A soft answer turns away wrath, but a harsh word stirs up anger*" (Proverbs 15:1). She carefully picked her timing, and went to meet David. When she arrived, she met him with a meal. She fed him, calmed him down, and got him to relax.

Ladies, how do you deal with the temper of a man who is going through a transition? A man who seems so far from his vision, one who is frustrated, broken, and seems to have lost his dream? How do you deal with a man when he doesn't have enough money? The answer is not the divorce court, nor packing your bags and going to your mother's house. You need to ask God to give you discernment and a wise tongue. Being a true woman of God is being able to speak with a wise tongue to a man in transition. You can be his dream restorer.

The first thing Abigail did when she met David was to honor him. Believe me, he didn't look like anything worth honoring. Here was a man who lived in a cave with six hundred rejects. He didn't have any possessions to his name; all he had was a promise from God. But she showed honor to that dirty, smelly, angry, unreasonable man.

> *And it shall come to pass, when the LORD has done for my lord according to all the good that He has spoken concerning you, and has appointed you ruler over Israel.* (1 Samuel 25:30)

In referring to him as *"lord,"* she acknowledged that she was in the presence of a king. David did not look like a king. He wasn't wearing a crown on his head, but Abigail said, in effect, "I believe what God says about you." She was using the Word of God to save her family and her future. She kept on using the Word, and it got inside David. It took away his temper. It took away his violence. It took away his anger.

Many times, we just don't want to use the promise God has given us—His Word. We would rather use our intellect and wit. We would rather use manipulation and control. That is why many marriages are unhappy—there is no love in the home. I dare you to ask God what He thinks about the person you are sleeping next to. Ask God what He says about your spouse. We give up too soon! You can either be a person of faith like Abigail, or a fool like Job's wife, who advised her husband to curse God and die. (See Job 2:9.)

God's Word is incapable of lying. So, keep talking about it until the Word becomes flesh. Remember to talk to the king in your man, and the king will stand up. Call out the queen in your wife, and the queen will emerge. David said, *"Blessed is the LORD God of Israel, who sent you this day to meet me! And blessed is your advice and blessed are you, because you have kept me this day from coming to bloodshed and from avenging myself with my own hand"* (1 Samuel 25:32–33).

There will be times in your life when you will feel like giving up on the dream God has given you. Before you destroy your destiny by doing something you will regret, God will always send the Holy Spirit, like He sent Abigail, to intercept you and remind you of what God has said about your future, *"For I know the thoughts that I think toward you, says the LORD, thoughts of peace and not of evil, to give you a future and a hope."* (Jeremiah 29:11)

BEING THE VOICE OF DISCERNMENT FOR OTHERS

Is there anyone in your life who is in transition? Like David, they are in that in-between place? They just can't seem to get where they are trying to go? Ask God to give you discernment and a wise tongue. You could be the voice of discernment, speaking the Word of God into their "unguarded moment," stopping them from throwing away their destiny. Anybody can believe in him- or herself when they are on top of the world, but those with the gift of discernment will speak out in the valley, calling things that are not as though they were. The discerning believer sees potential in people when they don't see it. Pray for God to give you the right words to speak to those in transition, to help restore their dreams.

> *Anybody can believe in him- or herself when they are on top of the world, but those with the gift of discernment will speak out in the valley, calling things that are not as though they were. The discerning believer sees potential in people when they don't see it.*

Nabal died a premature death three weeks later. David went on to become a great king. David eventually married Abigail. In saving David's future, Abigail also secured her own.

As I think back on my ministry, my mind races to the two or three critical moments when leaving seemed easier than staying. During one particularly hard time, I was greatly discouraged. Division was wreaking havoc in our church. Some people left, people whom I thought would never leave. It seemed the problems just kept on coming, one after another after another. Everything I had worked for felt like it was hanging by a thread. It was the darkest hour of my pastorate.

To make matters worse, while driving home one day, I rear-ended a car at a stop sign. Even though it was just a fender bender, it felt like I couldn't do anything right. When I walked in the door of my home, the phone rang. It was the person that I had rear-ended. His first question was, "Are you that guy who pastors that big church?" He informed me that, all of a sudden, his neck and back were hurting. A lawsuit seemed imminent. At that moment, something inside of me collapsed.

After dealing with the church problems for months, the straw that broke the camel's back broke mine, and I began to weep. I consider myself to be a strong, "can-do" person. I am not a quitter. But, at that moment, I had reached the end of my strength.

I will never forget how my wife instantly discerned my vulnerability. At that critical moment, she took control of the situation. She immediately got on the phone and dealt with the crisis, defusing it masterfully. She spoke confidently to me about my future. By the time she got through with me, I felt like I could whip a pack of lions.

How strange. I had always been the person giving hope and encouragement to others with my preaching. But this time, God wanted to encourage me.

I know without a doubt, had I not felt my wife's strength at the moment, had she not stood up to the crisis and become the discerning voice of God to me about my future, I would have left the ministry in defeat.

Never underestimate the power God has placed in you to discern the seasons your loved ones are experiencing. Don't drown out that voice on the inside, for it could be the voice that restores their dreams.

Now, years later, thousands of people attend any one of our Free Chapel multisite campuses. From our one hundred fifty-acre campus in Gainesville Georgia, to our West Coast campus in Irvine, California, God has used this ministry to reach more souls than I ever imagined. But it all teetered that afternoon on the discernment of my wife. When I reflect on the discernment and strength Cherise exhibited that day in my unguarded moment, I feel like David when he said to Abigail, in effect, "Blessed is the God of Israel who sent you to me to keep me from sinning." (See 1 Samuel 25:33.)

The Holy Spirit will speak to you when your family needs encouragement. Your tongue can make or break your loved ones. The impressions the Holy Spirit gives you about them are for a reason. Pray, and wait for the right time in their lives when God will open the door for you to speak to them. Discernment will let you know when to back off and give them some space, and when to speak up with the truth that has been revealed to you.

If my wife had put me down that day during my unguarded moment, I dare not think where our family or ministry would be today. I thank God that I had an Abigail in my life; I had a voice of discernment.

Take a moment now to stop and reflect on what you have read, and what it means to you and for your life. Consider each of the questions below and journal your answers. Date this page, so that when you look back, you will have a record of your journey in this season of life. Any time the Lord speaks to you, it is important to record it.

DATE: _____

CHAPTER 9 QUESTIONS:

1. List two key points that were discussed and give your understanding for each of those key points.

_____

_____

_____

_____

2. Based on what you have learned in this chapter, are there any areas of your life in which you will begin to act or think differently?

_____

_____

_____

_____

3. What would you consider to be unguarded moments in your life?

_____

_____

_____

_____

CHAPTER 9 CONCLUDING REFLECTION

Your reflection should include the following:

+ What you learned

+ What had the most value for you or had direct application to your life

+ Any other takeaways

_____

_____

_____

_____

_____

_____

_____

_____

_____

_____

_____

_____

_____

_____

_____

_____

_____

_____

_____

_____

_____

UNLOCKING DISCERNMENT WITH PRAYER

I will give you the keys of the kingdom of heaven.
—Matthew 16:19

Here is a precious secret I've learned: prayer invites angels into the war zone of your experience.

In Acts, King Herod imprisoned the apostle Peter, guarding him with four squads of soldiers. They were no match, however, for the prayers of the believers. *"Peter was therefore kept in prison, but constant prayer was offered to God for him by the church"* (Acts 12:5). And the result?

> *That night Peter was sleeping, bound with two chains between two soldiers; and the guards before the door were keeping the prison. Now behold, an angel of the Lord stood by him, and a light shone in the prison; and he struck Peter on the side and raised him up, saying, 'Arise quickly!' And his chains fell off his hands.* (Acts 12:6–7)

When you pray, God dispatches angels.

Jesus prayed in the garden of Gethsemane, and angels came and ministered to Him. (See Luke 22:43.)

Paul prayed in the midst of a storm, out in the middle of an ocean, and God sent an angel to stand by him. (See Acts 27:23.)

When you pray, God releases angels. No matter what you're going through, they stand by you. If this is true, then one of the greatest tragedies of prayerlessness is the scores of unemployed angels just waiting to be dispatched by God. Angels are attracted to the place of prayer.

Charles Haddon Spurgeon pastored the first mega-church of ten thousand members in London, England, back in the 1800s. His sermons were published and still inspire millions today. Although you've probably heard of Charles Spurgeon, I doubt very much that you've ever heard of James Spurgeon. James was Charles's brother and business manager.

Prayer builds a power base allowing you to do what God commands you to do.

When Charles Spurgeon took the pulpit at Metropolitan Tabernacle, James went under the pulpit, into a secret prayer closet. The key to Charles Spurgeon's powerful preaching was his brother's powerful praying. Prayer builds a power base allowing you to do what God commands you to do. We've seen the power of disagreement destroy churches and homes; it's time to see the power of agreement in prayer ignite our churches and homes, as well as revive us personally.

The greatest people on earth are people who pray. I don't mean people who talk about prayer, nor people who believe in prayer, nor even those who can explain prayer beautifully; I mean people who put in the time on their knees in prayer. These folks aren't necessarily blessed with spare hours to pray—they make the time by taking time away from less important things. Put prayer first and your schedule second. The prevailing prayer of faith is the power on earth that employs the power of heaven. Whatever you do after that is merely gathering up the results of prayer.

Prayer has brought hearing to the deaf, sight to the blind, life to the dead, salvation to the lost, and healing to the sick. Prevailing prayer should be the main business of our day.

Every day, we must pray! Do you take time to pray each day? Do you have a place where you meet God every day? What place does prayer hold in your life? And an even greater question: Do you believe your prayers matter? They do, my friend. They really do.

If prayer is anything, prayer is everything. If the church will not pray, God will not act. For Jesus said, *"I will give you the keys of the kingdom of heaven"* (Matthew 16:19).

PREVAILING PRAYER

What is prevailing prayer? It is not foxhole praying—praying only when you are in a crisis. It is not half-hearted, lukewarm, lay-me-down-to-sleep prayer. Prevailing prayer is wrestling against principalities and powers. Paul said, *"Therefore I exhort first of all that supplications, prayers, intercessions, and giving of thanks be made for all men"* (1 Timothy 2:1). It is the protracted prayer, fasting prayer, weeping prayer, effectual prayer, and fervent prayer of the righteous that avails much. (See James 5:16.)

The power of prevailing prayer is evident in James's account of the prophet Elijah influencing the weather with his prayers, *"Elijah was a man with a nature like ours, and he prayed earnestly that it would not rain; and it did not rain on the land for three years and six months. And he prayed again, and the heaven gave rain, and the earth produced its fruit"* (James 5:17–18). (See also 1 Kings 17.)

Prevailing prayer is Esther fasting for three days and saving her nation by causing the enemies of the Jews to be defeated. (See Esther 4:16.) That's prevailing prayer!

Prevailing prayer is Hagar interceding in prayer, *"Let me not see the death of the boy [Ishmael]"* (Genesis 21:16). God heard her prayer and blessed Ishmael because of the prevailing prayer of a mother.

Prevailing prayer is Rizpah, a concubine who bore two sons with King Saul. David gave the two boys to the Gibeonites to atone for Saul's treatment of them. The two boys were subsequently hung by the neck until they died. Afterward, the boys' remains were not cut down, but remained to be devoured by wild beasts. Rizpah, their mother, would not be satisfied with that. So, she took a piece of sackcloth and spread it upon a rock. For five months, she sat there in a vigil with nothing left but the bones of her boys. She used to adorn herself with silk in the king's court, but now, after months of sitting on a rock fighting for what was left of her family, I'm sure she was wild-eyed and haggard, like a lioness guarding her cubs. She didn't forsake them through the wind, rain, cold, or sun, not even through the attacks of the wild beasts and vultures. She would not give up on her children until they were cut down and let loose. (See 2 Samuel 21:10–14.)

Finally, word reached King David about what she was doing. He gave a command to bury the boys with Saul in graves belonging to kings. Scripture tells us that, *"They performed all that the king commanded. And after that God heeded the prayer for the land"* (verse 14). Because Rizpah prevailed, a king was moved, her sons were honored with burials in the tomb of kings, and God heard their prayers.

Prevailing prayer is having the tenacity to hold on until something happens. One of the greatest weaknesses of this generation is a lack of commitment for the long haul. The fastest animal on earth is the African cheetah. It has been measured at seventy miles per hour. However, the cheetah has one problem: it has a small heart, so it tires quickly. If it doesn't catch its prey quickly, it won't last. Some people have a cheetah approach to prayer. They lack heart to sustain the effort for the long haul. They burst out in prayer, but it doesn't last long. Why have a cheetah heart when God wants you to have an eagle heart? Isaiah 40:31 says, *"Those who wait on the LORD shall renew their strength; they shall mount up with wings like eagles, they shall run and not be weary."*

THE POWER OF EFFECTIVE PRAYER

Why is it that Christians often neglect prayer? I believe we do not understand the effect our prayers have in the spirit realm. As I was reading Revelation one day, some verses seemed to leap off the page:

> *Golden bowls full of incense, which are the prayers of the saints."*
>
> (Revelation 5:8)

> *The smoke of the incense, with the prayers of the saints, ascended before God.... Then the angel took the censer, filled it with fire from the altar, and threw it to the earth."*
>
> (Revelation 8:4–5)

What marvelous images! When you pray, you are filling the prayer bowls of heaven. In God's perfect timing, your prayers are mixed with the fire of God (His power) and cast back down to earth to change your situation. Your prayers don't just bounce off the ceiling; they rise like incense before the throne of God!

Even if you don't feel like anything is happening in the natural world, when you pray, you are filling the prayer bowls in the spirit realm. When they are full, they will tilt and pour out answers to your prayers!

A GENERATION IN PERIL

I believe that God is ready to tilt the prayer bowl on this generation. Today, there are more abortions in our country than ever before. Why is the devil trying to keep this generation from being born? I believe it is because God has something special in mind for this generation, and the devil knows it. The first generation Satan tried to keep from being born was Moses' generation. Pharaoh decreed that all the male children under the age of two were to be killed. Moses' generation was a deliverance generation.

The second generation Satan tried to eliminate was Jesus' generation. King Herod decreed that all the children, again under the age of two, were to be killed. This was another deliverance generation.

Now, Satan has staked his claim to a third generation—your generation. The reason there is such an attack on this generation through abortion is that you are destined to be a deliverance generation! No matter what kind of hell you're going through, you must prevail in prayer until you tilt the bowl in heaven.

Some time ago, I read the true story of a pilot in a small plane who had a warning light indicating an open door on the plane. He got up to check it out and, just as he got there, the door blew open and sucked him out of the plane.

The copilot radioed back to the tower, "I'm coming back. The pilot just got sucked out of the plane! Send rescue choppers to search for his body." What the copilot didn't know was, when the door flew open and pulled the pilot out, the emergency ladder fell—and clinging to it for dear life was the pilot.

In fifteen minutes, the copilot landed the plane, unaware that the pilot's head was only three inches from the concrete. When onlookers realized what was happening, they ran out onto the airstrip to help the pilot. They had to pry his fingers loose one finger at a time.

Prayer and discernment go hand in hand.
God is in need of men and women who will stand
in the gap and become prevailing prayer warriors.

Do you know what you call that? Perseverance! Hanging in there! Prevailing prayer is hanging in there until you fill the prayer bowls.

Prayer and discernment go hand in hand. God is in need of men and women who will stand in the gap and become prevailing prayer warriors. In 1 Timothy, Paul pleaded with the church, "*I desire therefore that the men pray everywhere, lifting up holy hands, without wrath and doubting*" (1 Timothy 2:8). In Acts, Paul had a vision in which a man was saying, "Come to Macedonia." When Paul arrived there he didn't find a man but, instead, found a group of women praying by the river. (See Acts 16:13.) Because of these women's prayers in Macedonia, Paul changed his direction. If those women had not been praying, Paul would not have gone west but east toward Asia.

Prayer, discernment, and service are the foundations on which the church is built. Prayer has been at the forefront of every major revival that has taken place on this earth.

PRAYER: AN INSATIABLE HUNGER FOR CHANGE

Proverbs 30:15–16 says,

The horseleach hath two daughters, crying, Give, give. There are three things that are never satisfied, yea, four things say not, It is enough. The grave; and the barren womb; the earth that is not filled with water; and the fire that saith not, It is enough. (KJV)

Horseleach is a strange word and is only used once in the entire Bible. It is a bloodsucker, a greedy thing that has an awesome appetite. It just can't get enough. This text says the horseleach has two daughters who cry, *"Give, give."* The double annunciation is important. This Scripture is saying there are four things that are never satisfied:

1. THE GRAVE

If you visit Arlington National Cemetery in Washington, DC, you will see white crosses as far as the eye can see. Thousands and thousands of soldiers have passed away, and yet the grave is still hungry. It still reaches up with grassy teeth, grabs men by the ankles, and pulls them down. The grave never gets enough. It doesn't respect old or young, male or female. It just keeps crying, "Give, give!"

2. THE EARTH THAT IS NOT FILLED WITH WATER

The ocean is fed by mighty rivers such as the Mississippi, the Nile, the Niagara, and the Amazon. Yet, with all the water flowing in from all over the world, the oceans never cover the earth. Water falls from the sky and rises up from the ground. Floods and rivers explode their banks, but the ocean never gets full. The ocean never gets filled with water. It just keeps crying and crying, "Give, give!"

3. FIRE

Think of the great fires of history: The Great Chicago Fire, the San Francisco Fire of 1906, or the Great Fire of London. Fire swallows up businesses, hotels, and homes. It's never becomes full. The more you put in its way, the more it takes. It's a horseleach. It keeps crying, "Give, give!"

4. THE BARREN WOMB

How can the writer of Proverbs compare the barren womb to a fire that is never satisfied, to the ocean that is never full, or to the grave that never has enough? What is God saying? The great lesson contained in here is this: God is not moved by gentle suggestion, nor is He moved by passive people. God is not shaken because we mumble a quick, little prayer. In the history of the Bible, all of the miraculous works of God were the result of incessant, enormous, insatiable hunger for change.

As thirsty as the ocean is to swallow up rivers and not be quenched, as hungry as fire is to eat up everything it can get and still look for fuel, as unsatisfied as the grave is to take in millions yet still cry daily for more, as insistent as a barren woman is that God give her children or she will die—that's how much we must desire to see the promises of God fulfilled. How do we birth God's will in the earth? We travail in prayer. The word *travail* expresses the pain and hard work of birthing a baby. No man knows about that word on the same level as a woman. Perhaps that's why they are so powerful in prayer.

In the history of the Bible, all of the miraculous works of God were the result of incessant, enormous, insatiable hunger for change.

As the ocean desires water, as fire consumes fuel, as the grave hungers for bones, so must the people of God crave a movement of God that bears souls and revival. When God gets ready to birth a promise, He looks for the barren soul who will cry, "Give, give!" He looks for sons and daughters of the horseleach!

In Genesis, Rachel was the true love of Jacob. Unfortunately, Rachel was barren and had to stand by and watch as Jacob fathered children by his other wives. Finally, the hunger of this barren woman could take no more as she pleaded with Jacob and with God, "*Give me children, or else I die!*" (Genesis 30:1). Eventually, after much travailing, "*God remembered Rachel, and God listened to her and opened her womb*" (verse 22). She gave birth to Joseph. Years later, Rachel bore a second son, Benjamin.

To whom will this revival be given? It will come to people who are hungry as a grave, thirsty as a river, and as ravenous as a fire. It comes to the congregation who never stops crying, "Give, give!" Prevailing prayer is Rachel praying, "*Give me children, or else I die!*" Oh, how we need men and women of prayer in the church again!

In the early days of the Christian church, the explosion of believers was threatening to bring it down. In the flesh, they just couldn't meet all the needs of the hurting. So the disciples called a meeting.

The twelve summoned the multitude of the disciples and said, "It is not desirable that we should leave the word of God and serve tables. Therefore, brethren, seek out from among you seven men of good reputation, full of the Holy Spirit and wisdom, whom we may appoint over this business; but we will give ourselves continually to prayer and to the ministry of the word. (Acts 6:2–4)

The apostles were torn between the work of the ministry and time spent in prayer. But they also knew that if they didn't give up on prayer, they wouldn't have to choose between the two—they could have both. They knew that ministry without prayer was powerless and ineffective. But it would take more than just the occasional prayer. They knew the stakes. They knew that they needed to devote themselves "*continually to prayer.*"

In Luke 18, we see the power of persistent prayer. Sometimes you just have to keep asking. In Jesus' parable, a widow appeared before a judge repeatedly, but her request fell on deaf ears. She didn't get discouraged; she didn't quit. You must be persistent. Finally, the woman persisted so long, the judge said, in effect, "I don't usually do this, and under normal circumstances I wouldn't. But I've got to do something for this woman or she's going to wear me out." (See Luke 18:1–5.) You have to become "a spiritual pest." Every time God looks up, let Him see you before Him.

You have to desire it so much that you tell God, "I'm going to wear You out. I'm going to keep praying until You save my children, until You bless my family. I'm going to stay in Your face. Jesus, I'm going to be a spiritual pest and wear You out. I'm not going to break down; I'm about to have a breakthrough."

A friend of mine named Tommy Tenney, author of *The God Chasers*, introduced me to a great woman of God. She has a reputation as a true prayer warrior. She and her husband started a church in Alexandria, Louisiana, where they established a prayer meeting that has never stopped. For over thirty years, twenty-four hours a day, there has been someone in that church praying.

Her son is now the pastor of this great church where thousands attend. Early on, she made God a promise concerning her son. She vowed to God that she would fast and pray on his birthday all the days of his life, from sunup to sundown. For over fifty years, on her son's birthday, she has gone to the church in the early hours of the day to shut herself away and pray all day for her son without food. As a result, he has become a great man of God.

When former President Bill Clinton first met her son, he was still the governor of Arkansas. He was so impressed with this minister that, even after becoming president, he would often fly into town just to attend his church for special services. Clinton invited her son to the White House several times to minister to the president, especially during turbulent times.

For over fifty years, that silver-haired mother prayed and fasted all day for her son on his birthday. Her persistence moved her son from the small, obscure town of Alexandria, Louisiana, all the way to the most powerful office in the world.

God is not looking for ability; He is looking for availability. You are part of an army that God is raising up to crush the enemy's skull. I feel God saying, "Get my people praying again. I'm going to use them in the final battle."

Take a moment now to stop and reflect on what you have read, and what it means to you and for your life. Consider each of the questions below and journal your answers. Date this page, so that when you look back, you will have a record of your journey in this season of life. Any time the Lord speaks to you, it is important to record it.

DATE: _____

CHAPTER 10 QUESTIONS:

1. List two key points that were discussed and give your understanding for each of those key points.

_____

_____

_____

_____

2. Chapter 10 talks about the importance of prayer in the life of a believer. Describe your prayer life in two to three sentences.

_____

_____

_____

_____

3. Please be completely honest and transparent on this question, and I promise you will receive *no* judgement from me: On a scale from 1–10 (10 being very effective and 1 being completely ineffective), describe the power you feel your prayers have.

_____

_____

_____

_____

4. What would it take to move that score closer to a 10?

_____

_____

_____

_____

5. Based on what you have learned in this chapter, are there any areas of your life in which you will begin to act or think differently?

_____

_____

_____

_____

CHAPTER 10 CONCLUDING REFLECTION

Your reflection should include the following:

+ What you learned
+ What had the most value for you or had direct application to your life
+ Any other takeaways

_____

_____

_____

_____

_____

_____

_____

_____

_____

_____

_____

_____

_____

_____

_____

_____

_____

_____

_____

11

DISCERNING WOMEN ALWAYS MAKE A DIFFERENCE

The Lord gave the word;
great was the company of those who proclaimed it.
—Psalm 68:11

One of Satan's greatest fears is that women will find out who they really are, and what a significant role they play in his ultimate downfall. The truth is, Satan is afraid of women because they are God's secret weapons for the final battle.

Why would God use women? I believe the answer is simple: the opening round of the battle was between the devil and a woman (Eve). Consequently, it is logical that the last round of this important final thrust should also include women.

The verse above depicts an army on the march, proclaiming the gospel. The biblical record shows that women have not been relegated to mere privates in God's army; they have been chosen as key players to transform the world. How fascinating it is that, even in the male-dominated Jewish culture, God made it a priority to include several discerning women as key figures in history.

DISCERNING WOMEN OF SCRIPTURE: DEBORAH

In Judges, the men of Israel hesitated when they received directions from God. Deborah, a prophetess, discerned God's instruction and decided to make a difference:

Then she [Deborah] sent and called for Barak the son of Abinoam from Kedesh in Naphtali, and said to him, "Has not the LORD God of Israel commanded, 'Go and deploy troops at Mount Tabor; take with you ten thousand men of the sons of Naphtali and of the sons of Zebulun; and against you I will deploy Sisera, the commander of Jabin's army, with his chariots and his multitude at the River Kishon; and I will deliver him into your hand'?" And Barak said to her, "If you will go with me, then I will go; but if you will not go with me, I will not go!" So she said, "I will surely go with you; nevertheless there will be no glory for you in the journey you are taking, for the LORD will sell Sisera into the hand of a woman." Then Deborah arose and went with Barak to Kedesh.   (Judges 4:6–9)

If you will decide to make a difference, then God will make up the difference. You have to believe in yourself, if only because God believes in you.

Two major things opposed Deborah that day. First, she was a woman in a male-dominated society. Second, she didn't have a sword with which to fight. But when Deborah got involved, God brought the army to her.

If you will decide to make a difference, then God will make *up* the difference. You have to believe in yourself, if only because God believes in you. You may feel inadequate to complete the task, but that's all right. Remember, God's supernatural involvement requires faith.

Deborah arose to lead God's people to victory over Sisera, the evil captain of the Canaanite army, who was reduced to running for his life. He ducked into a woman's tent to hide, thinking an ordinary housewife wasn't much of a threat to him. But while he was sleeping, this ordinary woman named Jael took a tent peg and drove it through his temple, killing him. (See Judges 4:17–21.) Think of what a surprise it must have been to hear the news that Sisera, the mighty warrior, had been slain by a housewife with a tent peg.

You can make a difference. God wants to raise up an army of housewives to proclaim His good news and defeat all His enemies that are coming against the family and the church.

In Genesis 33, when Jacob had to face his brother, Esau, after stealing the blessing, he was afraid for his life. Esau and four hundred of his soldiers were approaching with fire in their eyes. Do you know what Jacob did? He put all the women out in front and hid behind them. When Esau saw the women, he broke down and began to weep. (See Genesis 33:1–7.) The presence of women on the front line altered the spirit of the enemy.

Or, consider the New Testament account of the resurrection:

Now when the Sabbath was past, Mary Magdalene, Mary the mother of James, and Salome bought spices, that they might come and anoint Him. Very early in the morning, on the first day of the week, they came to the tomb when the sun had risen….Now when He rose early on the first day of the week, He appeared first to Mary Magdalene, out of whom He had cast seven demons. She went and told those who had been with Him, as they mourned and wept. And when they heard that He was alive and had been seen by her, they did not believe. (Mark 16:1–2, 9–11)

Here was the greatest single moment in the history of the world, and the only witness was a woman. This, to me, is ironclad proof that Scripture comes from God and not from men. In the Jewish culture, women had few rights. They couldn't teach or even become educated. Because of this, they were not allowed to testify in legal matters. Their voice meant nothing. If it were left to Jewish men to invent the Scriptures, they would have never left a woman to be the only witness of Jesus' resurrection. But God knew that only a discerning woman would be able to see and believe that, contrary to apparent circumstances, Jesus is alive!

WHO? ME?

Don't be ashamed if, when God calls your number, your first response is, "Who? Me?" If you've never said those words, then I suspect that God has never talked to you. Whenever we respond to God, saying, "I'm not able to do that," God responds back, "Well, good. Now that we've got that out of the way, are you ready?"

God is never drawn to full; He is only drawn to empty. In fact, more believers fail because of their strengths than because of weaknesses. The ironic message of Scripture is that there is weakness in strength and strength in weakness. (See 2 Corinthians 12:9–10.)

A mistaken notion in Christianity is that God is looking for strong people. Wrong! God is looking for weak people whose strength comes from Him.

The weakness of strength is found in the story of King Uzziah. He was sixteen when he began to reign. As long as he sought the Lord, God caused him to prosper. His fame spread far and wide. Then we come to a haunting phrase: *"But when he was strong his heart was lifted up, to his destruction"* (2 Chronicles 26:16).

A mistaken notion in Christianity is that God is looking for strong people. Wrong! God is looking for weak people whose strength comes from Him.

The strength of weakness always begins with brokenness. Paul was stoned and left for dead, an oozing mass of broken bones. He was broken internally. He was hurting emotionally, mentally, and physically. Paul was a broken man, but oh, the strength of weakness! When properly responded to, weakness always leads to graduated blessing. God's answer to Paul was, *"My grace is sufficient for you, for My strength is made perfect in weakness"* (2 Corinthians 12:9).

When is God's grace sufficient to help you? When you look around and there is nothing left but the grace of God. As long as something else remains, we will tend to place our trust in it.

Paul's response to God was, *"Most gladly I will rather boast in my infirmities, that the power of Christ may rest upon me"* (2 Corinthians 12:9). Stop looking at your weakness and begin to concentrate on His strength.

GOD'S ARMY OF BROKEN WOMEN

God is mobilizing and equipping a female army to build His church and do His work in these last days. Spiritual leaders and ministries across the country are rising up to host women's conferences. Bishop T. D. Jakes started teaching "Woman, Thou Art Loosed" in a Sunday school class. Later, it became a best-selling book, a conference, and a hit movie.

You might be surprised to learn what kind of women God is going to use in this end-time army. Only four women are mentioned in the genealogy of Jesus Christ. They are four of the "bad girls" of the Old Testament—Rahab was a harlot, Ruth was a former pagan and outcast widow with no right to marry an Israelite, Bathsheba was an adulteress, and Tamar was the widow who seduced her father-in-law. (See Matthew 1:3, 5–6.) It sure would seem that God could have found better women to make up the family tree of Jesus Christ!

You may not be all you ought to be, but, thank God, you're not what you used to be. If God could get you from where you were to where you are, then He can take you from where you are to where you ought to be!

I believe God deliberately chose these four women because He was trying to teach us about the power of redemption. After all, if women with that kind of past could be part of the physical family of Jesus Christ, then maybe the spiritual family of Christ, which is the church, can also include women with sordid pasts, now washed and cleansed by the blood of Jesus Christ.

You may not be all you ought to be, but, thank God, you're not what you used to be. If God could get you from where you were to where you are, then He can take you from where you are to where you ought to be! Don't let your past haunt you. Paul, who had a murderous history himself, told us, *"One thing I do, forgetting those things which are behind and reaching forward to those things which are ahead"* (Philippians 3:13). No matter your past, you can still reach for the future. God said through Isaiah, *"Do not remember the former things, nor consider the things of old. Behold, I will do a new thing, now it shall spring forth; shall you not know it? I will even make a road in the wilderness and rivers in the desert"* (Isaiah 43:18–19).

BREAKING FREE FROM YOUR SELF

You really can make a difference. But to become a discerning woman in God's army, you need to break free from the bondage of self-pity, self-loathing, and low self-esteem. Many things that happen to us in life can bind us in chains that keep us from being who God has called us to be. Our response can be to throw a pity party. We're called to walk through the valley, not wallow in it.

There are four steps to being set free:

1. TRACE IT.

When did it start? What events or attitudes from your past have contributed to your current state? It's time to get there and cut it out. Cut down the root if you want to get rid of the fruit. *"Even now the ax is laid to the root of the trees. Therefore every tree which does not bear good fruit is cut down and thrown into the fire"* (Luke 3:9).

2. FACE IT.

Admit to God and to people you trust that you have a problem. Simply say, "I need help, Lord; I'm struggling with this." Whatever has been locked away needs to be brought out into the light of day.

3. ERASE IT.

Let it all go. *"If we confess our sins, He is faithful and just to forgive us our sins and to cleanse us from all unrighteousness"* (1 John 1:9). Erase all sin and offense by applying the blood of Jesus Christ.

4. REPLACE IT.

Let the Holy Spirit fill the void. Ephesians 5:18 says, *"Be filled with the Spirit."* Renew your mind in the Word. Think God's thoughts, and ask God for a fresh baptism of Joy. Isaiah 61:3 teaches us to put on *"the garment of praise for the spirit of heaviness."*

Remember that God will always allow a little crisis to keep us dependent. The Lord will either calm your storms or calm you while the storm rages. God can turn every Calvary into an Easter, every midnight into a noonday, every sob into a sigh. Jesus will never allow you to drown in your own tears. He will not permit hurt to destroy your mind. He bottles every tear in His eternal container. *"You number my wanderings; put my tears into Your bottle"* (Psalm 56:8).

Right now, there are women reading these words who need to be set free from the bondage of self-pity. You are a child of God filled with His Spirit. Your name is in the Book of Life. The greatest issue in your life—the sin issue—has been settled. Your sins are under the blood of Jesus.

Say this out loud, right now:

I'm through feeling sorry for myself.
God wants me to be a victor, not a victim;
to soar, not sink;
to overcome, not be overwhelmed.

Nothing outside of us can cause depression, but our unbiblical response to things can.

In Jesus' name, I break you free from the bondage of self-pity.

BREAKING FREE FROM YOUR PAST

Ezekiel 18:2 says, *"What do you mean when you use this proverb concerning the land of Israel, saying: 'The fathers have eaten sour grapes, and the children's teeth are set on edge'?"*

This text refers to how the sins of parents affect their children. The sour grapes may be an abusive father or mother. Maybe your parents didn't know how to show love. Maybe they were absent or never available to you. Perhaps you could never do well enough for them. Possibly you never had any affection or affirmation. Sour grapes could be alcoholism, drug addiction, anger, negativism, or depression. These are some of the ways parents who eat sour grapes affect their children. A good reason to throw a pity party, right?

Wrong! Look at the next verse:

"As I live," says the Lord GOD, *"you shall no longer use this proverb in Israel."* (Ezekiel 18:3)

Good news! No matter who your father or mother is, no matter what their issues were, if Jesus is alive in you, then your parents' behavior no longer needs to become your stain. Jesus broke the curse.

No matter what sour grapes your parents ate,

no matter what they did wrong, it doesn't have to destroy your joy.

You don't have to be held hostage by

what they did to you or didn't do for you.

No matter what sour grapes your parents ate, no matter what they did wrong, it doesn't have to destroy your joy. You don't have to be held hostage by what they did to you or didn't do for you. So many people are dealing with issues that stem from past incidents of deep rejection, sexual shame, need for approval, never feeling good enough, or lack of self-worth.

No matter how your parents behaved, through Christ, the pain stops—sin's progression in your family line is broken. To the people who know their sovereign Lord lives, this sour grape proverb is defeated. Buddha and Muhammad can't break your family curse; neither one is alive. Our sovereign Lord is alive! In Jesus' name, I loose you from the bondage of family curse and sin.

The assignment God has for you is too great to be sabotaged by the past. Depression and lack of self-worth is illegal in your life. Life has done nothing to you that God can't use for good, if you will put it in His hands. God can turn your pain into purpose. It's time to make a difference.

THE SECRET TO LIFE TRANSFORMATION

You are already a success in the eyes of God. What is success? Don't fall for the world's faulty definition of success: fame and fortune. True success is knowing your worth in the eyes of God, and using your gifts properly. You may be thinking, *But you don't know how I have failed.* As Edwin Cole once said, "You don't drown by falling into the water; you drown by staying there."

The book of Romans tells us that the renewing of the mind is the secret to transformation. (See Romans 12:2.) What you see and believe in your mind, you will live out. Believe you are victorious. See yourself making a difference. If you know who you are, and Who it is that has called you, you will be able to endure anything. *"Who for the joy that was set before Him endured the cross"* (Hebrews 12:2). Jesus set his mind on the victory while He endured the crucifixion.

My mother-in-law, Pat, is a breast cancer survivor. My wife and I will never forget hearing the news. *Cancer* is a devastating word when it is attached to someone you love. After a few tears and a lot of prayer, Pat began to fight back. She refused to give up. Although the doctors recommended radical mastectomy surgery, she decided on the alternate route, a strict diet and immune-boosting vitamins.

I felt the call of God to fast three days for her healing. On the third day, God led me to share a word of encouragement with her: "You shall live to see your children's children." Pat has now been cancer-free for over twenty years! After going through such a storm, every day is like a gift. Today, she has turned her liability into an asset by encouraging other women with her testimony. Through the test came a testimony; from the mess came a message of hope for others walking through the emotional meat grinder of cancer.

The reason some people are never used by God is they have never been through anything. God gets His best sailors from the roughest seas and His fiercest soldiers from the toughest battles. God can use what you have experienced to bless others.

Such was the case in the life of Sylina LiBasci. I felt impressed to share with you a portion of her personal testimony about the most devastating day of her life:

> On May 16, 1997, I was being a mom as usual, and I got up early enough to have my devotion and pray. My four-year-old son, Caleb, came in, and I bathed him. Soon, my two-year-old Benjamin was awake, so I bathed him. I fed them breakfast while Wesli, my ten-year-old daughter, was dressing for the day.
>
> We were planning a day of fun at our church: water day at our Parents Morning Out class. I taught it on Fridays. The boys wanted to wear their "Jesus" shirts. These pictured Jesus with children and the Scripture from Matthew 19:14, which read, "Let the little children come to Me, and do not forbid them; for of such is the kingdom of heaven." They were so eager that morning. I had no way of knowing this would be our last morning together.
>
> On the way to church, a dump truck struck our car. My four-year-old, Caleb, went to be with Jesus instantly. Benjamin was critically injured and lived only two days and sixteen hours after the accident. My daughter, Wesli, was taken from the scene by helicopter to a children's hospital where, thankfully, she fully recovered from her injuries.

Though I will never fully understand why God chose to take my children, I can say God has turned my crisis into a miracle. The driver of the truck that struck us asked Jesus into his heart. Many doctors and nurses told us they would never be the same. But the greatest miracle occurred at the memorial service—where sixteen of our family members accepted Christ.

We had been praying for a household revival, and this was the beginning. God has opened the doors for us to minister to many grieving families. We have seen the Lord bind up the brokenhearted through our hardest life experience.

Although Sylina and her husband faced the greatest tragedy of their lives, God was able to bring something good out of it. Nothing can ever take the place of the children that she lost, but she takes comfort in knowing a difference has been made in the lives of others who are hurting and one day she will see them again.

I can promise you, hell is frightened that you're reading this book. New orders have come out of hell: "Don't let women catch a word of what's in that book. Don't let them understand what travailing prayer can do. Don't let them pick up on a spirit of discernment. Let the women stay so burdened with problems, so full of inferiority and self-pity, that they will never discover their gift of discernment and learn what a vital role they play in Satan's defeat."

The enemy fears praying, discerning women! They can break his authority over the home, over the family, over the husband, over the children. And when he's lost those battles, he's lost the war!

Take a moment now to stop and reflect on what you have read, and what it means to you and for your life. Consider each of the questions below and journal your answers. Date this page, so that when you look back, you will have a record of your journey in this season of life. Any time the Lord speaks to you, it is important to record it.

DATE: _____

CHAPTER 11 QUESTIONS:

1. List two key points that were discussed and then give your understanding for each of those key points.

_____

_____

_____

_____

2. For this question, please refer to the section of chapter 11 under the heading "Breaking Free From Yourself." Take a second look at the four steps to being set free. Restate, in your own words, what you think is being conveyed here.

_____

_____

_____

_____

3. Do you see yourself in any of those steps currently? Explain.

_____

_____

_____

_____

4. Based on what you have learned in this chapter, are there any areas of your life in which you will begin to act or think differently?

_____

_____

_____

_____

5. Who are the discerning women in your life?

_____

_____

_____

_____

6. What are some issues you need greater clarity or discernment about? Would you consider asking one of the women listed above?

_____

_____

_____

_____

CHAPTER 11 CONCLUDING REFLECTION

Your reflection should include the following:

+ What you learned

+ What had the most value for you or had direct application to your life

+ Any other takeaways

_____

_____

_____

_____

_____

_____

_____

_____

_____

_____

_____

_____

_____

_____

_____

_____

_____

_____

_____

_____

12

THE DISCERNING MAN
IS A REAL MAN

*Behold, I will send you Elijah the prophet
before the coming of the great and dreadful day of the* LORD.
*And he will turn the hearts of the fathers to the children,
and the hearts of the children to their fathers.*
—Malachi 4:5–6

What a powerful Scripture this is; it's really a warning. It may be the Old Testament, but the truth that it refers to affects us, particularly in this generation. It was saying, in effect, "Before the coming of the Messiah, there will be a turning of the hearts of the fathers back to their children."

There is a difference between being a male and being a man. Just because you're a male, that doesn't make you a man.

What is a real man? You don't measure a real man by muscles, but by moral fiber! You don't measure a real man by how successful he is in business, but by how successful he is at home! No amount of career success will compensate for failure at home. There's a difference between your reputation and your character. Reputation is who people *think* you are. Character is who your wife and your children *know* you are.

Real marriage has to go beyond moonlight and roses to daylight and dishes. Real marriage has to go beyond sex to sensitivity. Real marriage has to go beyond romance to responsibility. Statistics tell us that in homes where the father is a committed Christian, the children have a 75 percent chance of growing up to become committed Christians themselves. But in homes where only the mother is a committed Christian, that number drops to 23 percent. It's very obvious. God needs our males to stand up and become discerning men of God in the home.

When Joshua and the nation stood just across the river from their long-awaited promised land, God spoke to Joshua, saying in effect, "Joshua, tomorrow I'm going to take you across the river. Tomorrow, forty years of waiting is coming to an end; you're going to walk into a land flowing with milk and honey." But God had one last instruction for Joshua. *"Make flint knives for yourself, and circumcise the sons of Israel again the second time"* (Joshua 5:2). He was basically saying, "Sanctify them again." As every man surely knows, circumcision was a cutting of the flesh that designated Jewish men as set apart to be used by God. Now, before Israel could enter their Promised Land, God was calling for a re-sanctification.

BECOMING RE-SANCTIFIED

God was saying, "Unprecedented blessings are about to come to people in that church. But before I can take their families into all that I have prepared for them, I need the men to be re-sanctified. There needs to be a cutting away of fleshly things."

The truth is, you've been getting by while carrying some fleshly things. You've been doing some things thinking that God will just sort of wink at it—"Boys will be boys." But God is saying something different. He's saying, in effect, "This new thing I want to do requires a re-sanctification in every man's life. I want their eyes to be sanctified. I want their hearts to be sanctified. I want their minds and their spirits to be pure. I don't want them just coming to church and taking a secondary role in spiritual things in the home."

Circumcision, of course, was a cutting in those hidden, sensitive places. And that's just where men need it. We need to deal with those secret issues, those fleshly things that are hanging on to us, hindering us from receiving God's unprecedented blessings!

You probably know the story of Passover found in Exodus, where God took all the first-born of Egypt, but spared, or "passed over," the homes that had a marking on the door. In Ezekiel 9, there is an example of another Passover:

> The LORD said to him, "Go through the midst of the city, through the midst
> of Jerusalem, and put a mark on the foreheads of the men who sigh and cry
> over all the abominations that are done within it." To the others He said in my
> hearing, "Go after him through the city and kill; do not let your eye spare, nor
> have any pity…. But do not come near anyone on whom is the mark."
>
> (Ezekiel 9:4–6)

The application is this: God is saying, "If I can find men who will be burdened and cry out to Me for their wives and children, I'll save their families. But if there's not a man in that house who will carry the burden, then the destroyer will slay the women and the children."

I propose to you that we're living in just such days when the devourer is targeting our children and our wives. There may have been a time when you could get by with being secondary spiritually, with allowing your wife to do the praying and the Bible reading and the spiritual stuff, but we're living in an hour when I believe God is marking homes. He's saying, "There needs to be a man in every home that knows how to cry out, that knows how to pray for himself." Your pastor is not the spiritual head of your home, you are. And it's time for you to cry aloud. It's time for you to mark your home for the blessing.

GROW UP INTO DISCERNMENT

In 1 Corinthians 13:11, Paul said, *"When I was a child, I spoke as a child, I understood as a child, I thought as a child; but when I became a man, I put away childish things."* Notice that Paul uses *when* twice. There's the *"when"* of childhood and the *"when"* of manhood. He's not talking about your physical age, how many years you've been on this earth. There are some men out there who are locked in a protracted state of childhood. Children act like children. *"But when I became a man…"* It's time for some of you to grow up.

There comes a time, a rite of passage, when you move from childhood to manhood. People who know you should be able to look at you a year from now and see that you have bigger faith, bigger commitment, bigger prayer lives, and bigger dedication to God.

It's time for the men of God to grow up!
Hell has targeted your home and God is looking for
discerning men who will cry out to Him for their families!

Unfortunately, some men are stuck in spiritual childhood. You've been coming to church for a year, two years, maybe more, and by now, your children ought to see Daddy praising the Lord and discerning the things of God. Instead, you're still arguing about tithes, wondering whether you're going to go to church or not, and watching television or surfing the Internet instead of reading God's Word. I'm saying to you, man to man, it's time for the men of God to grow up! Hell has targeted your home and God is looking for discerning men who will cry out to Him for their families!

Notice, Paul said, *"I put away childish things."* He didn't say, "God took them away." Paul had to do some things for himself. God is saying, "I'm ready to mature you. I'm ready to take you to a new level!" In Malachi He said, in effect, "I'm going to turn the hearts of the fathers back to the children." There are wounds in us that only a father can cause; there are wounds in us that only a father can heal!

CURSE OF THE FATHERLESS

Kruger National Park in South Africa is the largest game preserve in the world. When they were facing an over population of elephants, they decided to separate the younger elephants from the older, more mature elephants because they were eating all the vegetation. So they took three hundred of the younger male elephants, separated them from the influence of the older, mature elephants, and moved them to South Africa's Hluhluwe-Umfolozi Reserve, three hundred miles away.

Hluhluwe-Umfolozi had no elephants but happened to be the natural terrain of the rare white rhino. The rhino has no natural enemies. It's not prey for anything. It's too mean, too tough; too fast; too strong. But to the amazement of authorities, they began to find dead rhinos all over the park. They couldn't figure out why. So they put cameras up and found that these young, male elephants, with no mature influence in their lives, were forming into packs and gangs to kill rhinos—something that was not in their nature.

Every night on the news, in every city in America, there are stories of gang violence. Do you know why we have gangs roaming? Do you know why we have killing and shooting? I believe it's because we don't have older, mature men who are speaking into the lives of our younger men, mentoring and developing and maturing and teaching them what is acceptable behavior and what is unacceptable.

Isaiah 4:1 gives a dire prediction: *"In that day seven women will take hold of one man and say, 'We will eat our own food and provide our own clothes; only let us be called by your name. Take away our disgrace!'"* (NIV). I believe this is a prophecy of the last days when there will be such a shortage of mature, discerning, godly men that women will come, seven women to one man, with their families, not for marriage or anything immoral, but for shelter, because they won't be able to find enough godly men to speak over their children and over their families' lives. Perhaps as the prophet said this, he foresaw our situation today, when 50 percent of the children in the U.S. are growing up in fatherless homes.

MEN AND WOMEN ARE DIFFERENT

If you know anything about biology, you know that when a man and woman conceive a child, the woman always provides an "X" chromosome because it's all she has. The male has both "X" and "Y" chromosomes. If he provides an "X," the child becomes a girl. If he provides a "Y," the child becomes a boy. The female doesn't have the ability to determine the sex of the child. It is the male that gives that identity to the child. If this is true in the natural world, think about the influence of a father to give identity to his children in the spiritual world. Nobody can speak into the life of our children like a man can. That's why it's so important for you to understand your role as a husband and father. A fatherless generation is being raised up but they've never been told who they are by a strong, male, godly voice!

Which chromosome we get makes so much difference in who we eventually become. Ladies, when you get that "X" chromosome you get a stronger immune system, and because of that you will live, on average, eight years longer than men. Studies prove that women fare better than men in concentration camps. Women withstand pain better than men. Women only deteriorate 2 percent every ten years, while men deteriorate 10 percent in the same time.

Men, on the other hand, have some benefits with their "Y" chromosome. Men carry a gallon and a half of blood in their bodies, compared to a woman's four-fifths of a gallon. A man has over one million more red blood cells per drop than a woman. That's why men have more physical strength.

Perhaps the greatest difference between men and women is in how our brains are wired. At conception, men and women are basically identical. But after a few days, men are washed by the chemical testosterone. The moment this chemical hits the brain of the male child, it instantly destroys some of the connecting fibers between its left and right side. However, an equivalent testosterone wash does not occur in the developing female's brain, and the left and right sides of her brain stay connected. This shows that men are literally brain damaged at birth! This frying of some of the connective fibers between the right and left side of the brain causes the man to be linear in his thinking. He uses only one side of the brain at a time. It's a medical fact.

Women think using both sides of the brain. They're like radar all the time, noticing everything. Men, on the other hand, are more logical, trying to make A plus B equal C. Women, on average, are more sensitive than men, sensitive to sound and light, as well as emotions.

Men use the left side of the brain most of the time. This is the side of the brain that is challenge-oriented, focused on objectives and goals. The right side of the brain is more feeling-oriented, nurture-oriented. It is better at remembering.

My point is this: God made us different for a reason. As great and gifted as women are, we need the influence of men in our homes, as well, to provide balance, stability, and protection. If you're a single mother, you need your church to provide strong male leadership for your children. The Lord said, "*Turn the hearts of the fathers to the children*" (Malachi 4:6). But He's also saying, "I need some men who'll carry a burden, some men who will be willing to say, 'Lord, I'm yours.'"

THERE'S A DAD IN THE HOUSE

Men, if a young man is coming to date your daughter, your silence is consent. Put down the remote control; turn off ESPN. You need to meet him at the door. He needs to know that this girl he's with has a daddy who's going to be watching. You need to look him in the eye and say, "Who are you? Who are your parents? What church do you go to? Where are you going to eat? And what time exactly will you be leaving and what time will you be home?"

You need to go down to the school and meet the principal and the teachers. They need to know that there's a daddy that cares. That's what a father does. There's more to being a man than having a zipper on your pants and bringing home a paycheck. Anyone can do that.

Men, we've gotten lazy and lethargic. We must get into their world! We must know what's going on! We've got to develop our spiritual discernment in order to feel when things aren't right in our household!

If your marriage is going to pieces and you're growing more and more distant, you need to open up your mouth and communicate. You need to say something. You need to do something to break the ice. You need to reach out; that's what men do. To be manly is to be godly.

If you're silent, then God will be silent.
But if you'll start praying, God will start moving.
If you'll start speaking, God will start speaking.

Why are you so quiet? Open up your mouth and talk to God about your family. Talk to Him about your marriage. To be silent is to give consent. If you're silent, then God will be silent. But if you'll start praying, God will start moving. If you'll start speaking, God will start speaking. Use your voice and speak into your family blessing, identity, and anointing in Jesus' name. Stand up and say, like Joshua, *"As for me and my house, we will serve the* LORD*"* (Joshua 24:15)!

THE SPIRIT OF A MAN

Proverbs 20:27 says, *"The spirit of a man is the lamp of the* LORD*; searching all the inner depths of his heart."* I have always interpreted that Scripture to mean that when God leads us, He does so through our spirits. He doesn't talk to our minds; He talks to our spirits, because *"the spirit of a man is the lamp of the* LORD*."*

This verse always makes me wonder, *What kind of light does my spirit give off?* That's a question we all need to ask ourselves, especially since our spirits are the lamp of the Lord. God, who is light, says, in effect, "The only light I have on earth to invade the darkness is the spirits of men and women."

In 2 Samuel 16, we find the story of David, whose throne has been overthrown by his son, Absalom. Scripture tells us,

> *Now when King David came to Bahurim, there was a man...whose name was Shimei the son of Gera, coming from there. He came out, cursing continuously as he came. And he threw stones at David and at all the servants of King David. And all the people and all the mighty men were on his right hand and on his left. Also Shimei said thus when he cursed: "Come out! Come out! You bloodthirsty man, you rogue!"* (2 Samuel 16:5–7)

David and his thirty mighty men were leaving their homes and their families, running for their lives. They were leaving everything they owned behind. These were warriors, but they were angry and embarrassed because not only have they lost everything, but now this little pipsqueak named Shimei threw rocks and cursed them as they left town.

One of the men turned and pleaded with David, *"Why should this dead dog curse my lord the king? Please, let me go over and take off his head!"* (2 Samuel 16:9). You can almost see the veins popping on his forehead, his hand on the shaft of his sword, just dying to go and take care of the nuisance. But David said,

> *Let him alone, and let him curse; for so the* LORD *has ordered him. It may be that the* LORD *will look on my affliction, and that the* LORD *will repay me with good for his cursing this day.* (verses 11–12)

David said, in effect, "This could be God checking me out, taking His lamp and putting it on my spirit to see what kind of spirit I really have."

Power withholding itself is far greater than power exerting itself. A Man proved that on a cross two thousand years ago. As He was arrested in the garden of Gethsemane, Jesus could have called down ten thousand angels, but He refused to do so. (See Matthew 26:53.) Imagine David looking at this little man who wasn't worthy to shine his shoes and basically saying, "I believe God is checking out my spirit in this situation."

THE TRIAL OF PRESSURE

There will be times when God will allow trial, complaint, and maybe even false accusation to come into your life. At that moment, God will take His lamp and put it to your spirit. You may be stronger and have more power and influence than your accuser. You may be able to crush him. But God knows that who you are under pressure is who you are. God wants to see if you have the right spirit in the face of adversity. God wants to know if you are able to *"bless those who curse you, and pray for those who spitefully use you"* (Luke 6:28).

It is in times of pressure, times of crisis, that your real spirit will come out. I love to walk with men who possess a good spirit. You may not be perfect. You may mess up. You may do things wrong. But God always goes beneath the surface to illuminate our spirits, saying, in effect, "I want to see how much light you're putting off by your spirit." No matter what happens to you in life; no matter who hurts you; no matter who cuts you off in traffic or undermines you at work; no matter what happens in your marriage or in your home, you need to have God's spirit, not a bitter, unforgiving, and angry spirit.

THE SPIRIT OF JESUS

The night before the crucifixion, an argument arose between the apostles as to who would be the greatest in heaven. (See Luke 22:24.) It wasn't the first time this argument had arose. (See Luke 9:46.) Then, knowing He was going to the cross in the next twenty-four hours, Jesus got up, took a basin of water and a towel, and went around the table, washing the feet of His disciples. (See John 13:4–5.) He even washed the feet of Judas who was about to leave to betray Him. I can't imagine what I would have done when I came to Judas, knowing, as Jesus did, of his upcoming betrayal. I probably would have yelled at Judas, pleaded with him, or restrained him. Instead, Jesus washed the feet of the man who would sell Him out. Jesus was demonstrating for them, beyond what words could ever say, the spirit of a servant. Then He instructed them, *"If I then, your Lord and Teacher, have washed your feet, you also ought to wash one another's feet"* (John 13:14).

"The spirit of a man is the lamp of the LORD." How much light do you give off by your spirit, by your attitude, and by who you are on the inside? Are you angry and bitter? Do you have that kind of spirit? Or, do you project the Spirit of Jesus?

Scripture says that when we get to heaven, God will judge *"the spirits of just men made perfect"* (Hebrews 12:23). That word *perfect* doesn't mean you are perfect; it means you are *mature* in Christ. It means, even when people curse you, you move on. When you have the chance to get back at someone who has really tried to do you harm, you hold back. I don't care how much people offend you; you need to get over it. The desire of the heart of a man of God says, "Make me like Jesus. Give me the spirit of forgiveness. Give me the spirit of purity. Give me the spirit of holiness. Give me the spirit of love. Give me the Spirit of Jesus."

Take a moment now to stop and reflect on what you have read, and what it means to you and for your life. Consider each of the questions below and journal your answers. Date this page, so that when you look back, you will have a record of your journey in this season of life. Any time the Lord speaks to you, it is important to record it.

DATE: _____

CHAPTER 12 QUESTIONS:

1. List two key points that were discussed and give your understanding for each of those key points:

_____

_____

_____

2. Based on what you have learned in this chapter, are there any areas of your life in which you will begin to act or think differently?

_____

_____

3. Who are the discerning men in your life?

_____

_____

_____

4. What are some issues you need greater clarity or discernment about? Would you consider asking one of the men listed above?

_____

_____

_____

CHAPTER 12 CONCLUDING REFLECTION

Your reflection should include the following:

+ What you learned

+ What had the most value for you or had direct application to your life

+ Any other takeaways

_____

_____

_____

_____

_____

_____

_____

_____

_____

_____

_____

_____

_____

_____

_____

_____

_____

_____

PART IV

BENEFITS OF DISCERNMENT

13

LIVE WITH GREAT EXPECTATION

And, behold, there was a man in Jerusalem whose name was Simeon, and
this man was just and devout, waiting for the Consolation of Israel, and
the Holy Spirit was upon him.
—Luke 2:25

In this chapter, I would like to challenge your thinking. There is knowing that God *can* do something and then there is the more courageous stance in the Lord in which you believe He *will* do something. But I am here to tell you there is an even bolder position to take. The boldest of all positions is expecting God will do something for you—specifically.

The farmer who believes God can bring rain prays for rain and then goes about his normal routine. The farmer who prays for rain and expects God to answer that prayer is the farmer who goes out and prepares the fields for rain. Sometimes when we think we hear from God, we move out with great expectation. We might even see confirmation after confirmation that tells us we are on the right path. But, inevitably, discouragement can come when we do not see more immediate results, or when progress seems to slow to a halt. It is in these moments that, if we aren't careful, we allow doubt to creep in, which is followed by a desire to throw up our hands and quit. In contrast, the Bible teaches us that when God gives promises—and He has—we are to be a people who live with great expectation.

GOD SPEAKS TO YOU IN GOD'S HOUSE

I'd like to take you back to when Jesus was born. The angels announced His birth to the shepherds in the field. They announced it to shepherds because shepherds know sheep and Jesus was the Lamb of God. It made sense for shepherds to be the first people to whom God would reveal that the Lamb of God, Jesus Christ, was born. Shepherds were also the ones to choose which sheep was to be offered as a sacrifice. These shepherds in the field were sent to the manger to verify that He was the Lamb of God from the very beginning.

When Jesus was only a few weeks old, His parents brought Him to the temple. (See Luke 2:22.) As parents, I think we wait too long to get our children involved in church. I'm afraid that too many parents only get concerned for their kids when they're cussing, drinking, and running with the wrong crowd. But notice the pattern that Mary and Joseph laid out. Jesus had only been alive for a few weeks, yet they said, "We have to get Him to church!" Even as an infant, they believed there was a blessing that would come on that child if He was in church. They wanted prophecy spoken over Him. They wanted hands laid on Him. They wanted the blessing spoken over Him. And so do you, for your children, no matter how young or old they are.

Cherise and I have five children and two grandchildren, so we understand the way life can tug on you and pull you in every direction. I can remember when the kids were small it would feel almost overwhelming to get everybody together and dressed and ready for church. Do it anyway. Take those kids to church. Even if they disagree or give you one hundred reasons why they have more important things to do; take those kids to church! You need to get back to that kind of seriousness about God's house.

Going to church is not playtime. It is not something that we do if we don't have anything else that we really want to do. There is life in God's house. There is peace and rest in God's house, and you can't tell me you couldn't use some rest when you are raising children. Church is where God works miracles for families. Start the pattern and habit of getting to God's house every week from the very beginning, even when they are just infants. If Mary and Joseph felt like they had to take Jesus to the temple just weeks after He was born, then how much more do we need to get our kids in church too? We need to get some prophecy spoken over our children. We need blessings spoken over that child. We need the Word spoken over our children and His Word spoken into the lives of our children. Nothing activates their gifts more than when they're in God's house, being taught about Jesus.

In Luke chapter 2 we are introduced to an old man by the name of Simeon. He was not a prophet, he was not a king, and he was not a priest. Simeon was a normal, everyday person, but the Bible considered him to be important enough to include his story. The Bible says that Simeon was a "*just*" man, which meant he was fair and honest, and that he was "*devout,*" meaning he was morally clean. More importantly, he had the ability to hear the Holy Spirit. Isn't it interesting that the name *Simeon* means "to hear," which meant that Simeon had the ability to hear the Holy Spirit? He could hear the spirit world. When God's voice, and God's Word, and God's promise went out, he could pick up on it. He could hear it.

> *And behold, there was a man in Jerusalem whose name was Simeon, and this man was just and devout, waiting for the Consolation of Israel, and the Holy Spirit was upon him. And it had been revealed to him by the Holy Spirit that he would not see death before he had seen the Lord's Christ. So he came by the Spirit into the temple. And when the parents brought in the Child Jesus, to do for Him according to the custom of the law, he took Him up in his arms and blessed God and said: "Lord, now You are letting Your servant depart in peace, according to Your word; for my eyes have seen Your salvation which You have prepared before the face of all peoples, a light to bring revelation to the Gentiles, and the glory of Your people Israel." And Joseph and His mother marveled at those things which were spoken of Him. Then Simeon blessed them, and said to Mary His mother, "Behold, this Child is destined for the fall and rising of many in Israel, and for a sign which will be spoken against (yes, a sword will pierce through your own soul also), that the thoughts of many hearts may be revealed."*
>
> (Luke 2:25–35)

The Holy Spirit told Simeon something very important about this baby Jesus. Because the Holy Spirit is a person, the Holy Spirit knows how to talk to you about your situation. The Holy Spirit knows how to talk to you about your future, and He desires to build into you that spirit of great expectation for something that is coming.

In the Old Testament, the Holy Spirit would come upon men in order to proclaim something specific, and then the Spirit would lift again. This man, Simeon, because of his unusual fellowship and relationship with God, his unusual relationship with the Holy Spirit, was not afraid of the Holy Spirit. He knew how to entertain the presence of the Holy Spirit, and the Holy Spirit would occasionally come upon him, and speak to him. And that is what the Holy Spirit wants to do with you. Simeon was not afraid of spiritual things. In this day and age, it's very easy to dismiss the voice of God in your life. But God is still speaking, and He is still looking for people whom He can talk to, people who can receive His promises. He is looking for people who are listening for His voice, sometimes through signs and wonders but more often than not, through His still small voice.

I have felt the Holy Spirit speak to me in such significant ways. It was a very powerful experience—one not to be taken lightly. Even as I was writing this chapter, the Lord spoke to my heart about something in my life, and I was astounded and astonished at how clear and precise it was. When He speaks, you don't have to wonder, *Did He really speak to me?* When He speaks, it's so specific that it will astound you. You may be down and depressed, but when you get a promise from the Holy Spirit, you begin to live with great expectation.

> *When God speaks, it's so specific that it will astound you.*
> *You may be down and depressed, but when you get a promise*
> *from the Holy Spirit, you begin to live with great expectation.*

I think the reason so many Christians don't live with great expectation is because they don't have God's Word in them. The reason so many Christians are depressed, discouraged, or even bored with their Christian life is that they don't understand what the Bible has to say about who they are, whose they are, and what their mission on earth is. When you get the Word in you, the Word will cause great expectation to come back to your life.

GOD'S MIRACULOUS TIMING

I believe the word of the Lord to you is that you need to live with great expectation, because everything He's promised, He's going to bring to pass in your life. I don't need to know who is reading these words right now, I only need to know that the Lord inspired me to write them and that He will bring those He is calling to read them. You are not reading this by accident or coincidence. The Holy Spirit has given you a promise. Be like Simeon and stay the course. *Stay the course.*

When God sets a promise in motion in your life, it's coming toward you, and what's coming toward you is worth waiting for. It's worth crying for. It's worth being alone for a season, if that's what it takes. It's worth going through the highs and the lows. It's even worth the criticism and the attacks. What God has coming is amazing and worth the fight. Live with great expectancy because what He's going to do in your future will astound you.

God didn't put you on this earth to kill time and He didn't create you just to be a space taker. *He put you here to be a difference maker.* God's not through with you—and this promise is not just for the young. I don't care who you are and how long it's been. Live with great expectation that God's not through blessing you. Habakkuk 2 is one of my favorite Scriptures. It says though the vision tarries, wait for it. *"It will not lie. Though it tarries, wait for it; because it will surely come, it will not tarry"* (Habakkuk 2:3). The Holy Spirit will never give you a word or a promise that He doesn't give you the ability to wait for.

Every miracle God does is within a time frame. Miracles are based on timing and timing is attached to every miracle. You don't want to be in Florida when God is fulfilling the miracle in Georgia. You don't want to be at Walmart when the Holy Spirit has your miracle at your church. You must be sensitive to the Spirit of God. Miracles are based on your being sensitive to the Spirit of God, because every miracle is dependent on your obedience.

I have a question for you: are you willing to risk looking foolish? Are you willing to say, "If that's what it takes, I'll do it!" Sometimes the miracle can only begin when you have reached your end. Are you willing to humble yourself and declare to God, "Not my will but Yours?"

RECOGNIZING YOUR MOMENT OF OPPORTUNITY

There is a synchronization of the Holy Spirit when He's working on one side of the miracle while, at the same time, He is also working on the other side—the side of things you cannot see from where you stand. The synchronization of when He's telling you that He's going to do something in you, and you get this feeling of great expectancy that something's going to happen. Maybe you're single and you're all by yourself and you get this feeling that the lonely years are over. You say, "The time that I've been alone was good, but I'm ready now, Lord, and I feel something moving." And God will be working on the other person at the same time, wherever they are. If they're in India, if they're in Australia, wherever they are, God is moving in their heart just like He's moving in yours.

Have you ever seen the incredible precision and flow of a synchronized swimming team? That's how the Holy Spirit works. He has you moving, and He has other things moving. God is orchestrating these divine arrangements, and you need to live with great expectancy that He has a plan. Don't you dare get depressed and discouraged, and don't you dare start talking defeat. God is not through with you. There is a moment coming when He will hook everything together. He will unfold His purpose. There is a day coming when you will collide with destiny.

I remember one of the big doors that God opened for me in a moment of destiny. Many years ago, when we were just establishing Free Chapel, I was asked to play my saxophone on the Trinity Broadcasting Network. They liked it so much that they invited me back, again and again. Now this was fine and I appreciated the opportunity, but I was more than just a sax player. I was a preacher and I was a pastor, too, but they never let me preach on the air. They just wanted me to play my saxophone. Then, one day, God's promise aligned with His timing, and something happened. I was at TBN getting ready to play my sax on the live show when the pastor who was supposed to preach that night became ill and couldn't even make it to the studio. During the live show, the producer told me what was happening and, lo and behold, here came the moment I had only hoped for: they asked if I would preach!

Don't you dare get depressed and discouraged, and don't you dare start talking defeat. God is not through with you. There is a moment coming when He will hook everything together.

I had to borrow somebody's Bible—I didn't even have my own with me. I grabbed this unfamiliar black Bible, and had no idea what I was going to preach on. There's nothing like going live on TV around the world without even having a note in front of you. But it didn't matter, because when God ushers you into your destiny, He will supply you with exactly what you need for that moment—many times *in* that moment. I just started preaching, and whatever I preached, it just started flowing. The next thing I knew, they were booking me for additional shows. Don't tell me God doesn't have moments for you just like He did for me! Believe in God for miracles of opportunity and thank Him that they are on their way right this moment.

Let me tell you about another moment of opportunity. The CFO of our ministry is named Tim Kernen. He and his wife, Sandy, were living in Tennessee, where Tim had a good full-time job. Our church was small at that time, but it was really growing, and we desperately needed help in our financial department. I had known Tim for some time and knew all of his great qualifications, so I contacted him and said that we really needed him to come help us. Tim told me that he and his family were secure and happy where they were. But even with all that, Tim agreed to pray about it. They had kids in school so this would be a major move for them. But Tim made the mistake of praying the riskiest prayer he could have prayed: "Lord, we'll do anything You want us to do, but You've got to speak to us. If we're supposed to go, just show us. We only want to do Your will."

Not long after he and Sandy prayed, they were talking in the car as they came to a stop light. One of them said, "Lord, we need You to show us a sign that will tell us if we are supposed to stay where we are or make this major move." Another mistake! No sooner had they said that prayer when, right in front of them, a van drove across the intersection, and on its side it read "Free Chapel."

Our worship leader at the time, James White, and his wife had gone to Tennessee in one of our church vans and they just happened to be at that same intersection where Tim and Sandy were praying for a sign. Tim said he looked over at Sandy and said, "Am I going crazy? Did I just see what I think I just saw?" Sandy excitedly responded that she saw it, too, and declared, "Let's go pack our bags. We're moving to Georgia!" They've been here ever since. Don't tell me God can't give you supernatural guidance and arrangements!

During the time Tim has been here, we have opened four additional campuses in several states and he has played a significant part in helping us steward the finances of the ministry each step of the way. We are so glad Tim and Sandy felt led to follow God's guidance and that they were willing to step out in faith. God can do the same for you!

Simeon had waited, and waited, and waited. When he finally got to the door of the temple and saw the Child he had been waiting for, he didn't even ask the parents, "Can I hold your child?" He grabbed baby Jesus, took Him in his arms, and blessed Him. When my moment came at TBN, I could have panicked in that TV studio and said, "Oh my God! I don't have any outlines. I'm not ready for this. I'm too nervous." No! Something within me said, *Seize this moment! If I fail, at least I'll know I tried.* I'd rather shoot for the moon and hit the stars than shoot for nothing and live the rest of my life filled with regret over opportunities not taken.

When your moment comes, and it *is* coming, reach out and grab it. Go for it. Don't make excuses. Don't insist that somebody else can do it better. If God wanted somebody else, He would have put them there. He wants *you.*

When Simeon came to that moment of opportunity, he obeyed. He prophesied that this child would be a light to the Gentiles and a blessing to His people. This child would be the one who is the Messiah. Today Simeon is listed among the great messianic prophets, like Isaiah and Ezekiel. What about you? Are you going to fulfill your purpose on earth? Like Simeon, you will not see death until the promise comes to pass. In other words, God is setting up appointments. Words from the Lord will keep you alive. Words from the Lord will keep your faith alive. Words from the Lord are constantly hitting your spirit and they are sent by God to keep your miracle alive. Feed that word. Feed that dream. Feed on the Word of God, because the Word of God will not return void. It will produce what has been promised. (See Isaiah 55:11.) When God says move, move. When God says wait, wait. He will make it all come together. He makes it all work out.

YOU WON'T SEE DEATH UNTIL YOU SEE OPPORTUNITY

One Sunday a few years ago, I stood in the back of the church, shaking people's hands as they were leaving the service. Earlier that morning, as I was preaching, my eyes had been drawn to a young man who was crying. Because of the Lord's prompting, I felt led to speak into this man's life. As I did, he broke down weeping. After the service, I noticed his whole family was gathered around him. I went over to them and they told me that this young man was a backslidden preacher who had gone down the wrong road in life but had recently returned home. That morning he had walked down the aisle and recommitted his life. You know what he said? He said, "I'm going to Bible school. I'm going back. I'm living with great expectation. I'm going to fulfill the call of God on my life."

After that, I shook hands with a young woman who told me her story. In 2002, a year after being married, she and her husband were told that they couldn't have kids due to her genetic health issues. Each year she had been praying and fasting, believing that God would give her a child. In 2004, at our old church, someone had prophesied over her and told her, "God spoke to me in my spirit and told me that you would have a son one day, and that you are to name him Simeon." Each year since, she kept fasting, believing, and praying. Each year, God gave her another nugget of hope. She told me, "Every time God has spoken to me I was in a service in this church. In 2012—I remember the date because it was 12/12/12—I was here on a Wednesday night, two days from undergoing a partial hysterectomy. We were registered for the surgery that Friday, December 14. But that Wednesday night, God clearly spoke to me and told me to cancel the surgery. I went home and told my husband. He thought I was crazy, but he agreed and I cancelled the surgery. A week and a half later, I found out I was pregnant."

I asked her to retell her story for our eleven o'clock service that morning. After she shared it, it was my honor and my privilege to introduce the most beautiful three-year-old you've ever seen: Terri Simeon Marshall! I thought the roof was going to lift off the building when the crowd rose to their feet and cheered. Isn't that great? I love that.

Don't let the enemy tell you that it's too late. You shall not see death until you see the promise. Live with great expectation. There's a spirit of depression on a lot of people who need the Word and the promises activated so that they can live with great expectation. And so do you. Good days are coming in your life. Powerful days. Anointed days.

Our God is a God of miracles and a God of breakthrough. He knows how to move in your family and in your life. Maybe you need a change today, a complete turnaround. Or possibly you need something that you don't yet have. Whether there's a void or an emptiness in your life and you just need hope, you can get it right with God right now. You can live with great expectation and stand on His promises. His voice will speak to you and remind you that greater things are yet to come. *"I know the plans I have for you,"* it says in Jeremiah 29:11 (NIV), *"plans to prosper you and not to harm you, plans to give you hope and give you a future."*

I believe that for many of you reading this book today, this is a "Simeon moment" for you. Simply obey the voice that you're hearing on the inside. Just obey it. Stay the course. I declare freedom over you. I declare healing over you. I declare miracles over you. I declare provision over you and the help that you need. I declare divine arrangements and connections from heaven for your life.

You're going to make it, and you're going to see the goodness of the Lord. The Lord's word to you is live with great expectation. It doesn't matter what's happened before today. It doesn't matter if you've failed. I believe God is saying to you, "I know who you are, and I have good things for you in your future. You are forgiven. Live with great expectation."

Take a moment now to stop and reflect on what you have read, and what it means to you and for your life. Consider each of the questions below and journal your answers. Date this page, so that when you look back, you will have a record of your journey in this season of life. Any time the Lord speaks to you, it is important to record it.

DATE: _____

CHAPTER 13 QUESTIONS:
1. Give a brief summary of your reading from chapter 13.

_____

_____

_____

_____

2. List two key points that stood out to you.

_____

_____

_____

_____

3. Describe how the voice of God spoke into your life in chapter 13.

_____

_____

_____

_____

4. Based on what you have learned in this chapter, are there any areas of your life in which you will begin to act or think differently?

_____

_____

_____

_____

5. Do you believe you are a person who lives with great expectation? Why or why not?

_____

_____

_____

_____

6. List three things you have great expectation for.

_____

_____

_____

_____

CHAPTER 13 CONCLUDING REFLECTION

Your reflection should include the following:

+ What you learned
+ What had the most value for you or had direct application to your life
+ Any other takeaways

_____

_____

_____

_____

_____

_____

_____

_____

_____

_____

_____

_____

_____

_____

_____

_____

_____

_____

_____

_____

_____

_____

14

DISCERNING SEXUAL TEMPTATION

For this is the will of God, your sanctification:
that you should abstain from sexual immorality.
—1 Thessalonians 4:3

I suggest that every parent reading this book share this chapter with their teenagers. We are living in a society where young girls and boys are asked to become adults overnight. Many young people have been trained to think that once they have sex, they will be "real" men and women; until then, they are merely little boys and girls.

"Girls Gone Wild" seems to be the moral theme of our current times. The twisted sexual images pop culture continues to produce, promoting everything from homosexual experimentation to casual sex, are in direct contradiction with God's Word.

The negative influences of the media, music, movies, and fashion magazines are brainwashing a generation of young men and women into believing it is perfectly normal to be sexually active before marriage.

"It's no big deal," "Everyone does it," "It can't be wrong if it feels so right," are the responses of men and women, young and old, who are making wrong decisions that seem right to them. Proverbs 14:12 says, *"There is a way that seems right to a man, but its end is the way of death."*

You must remember that even "good Christians" are not exempt from temptation. Often it is the "good" kids, kids who say they know sexual intercourse is wrong, asking, "How far can I go sexually?" When it comes to sexual integrity, most people want a list of dos and don'ts. What they really want to know is, "What can I get away with?"

What is the answer to, "How far can I go sexually?" It depends on your destination. The destination determines the route. If you want to reach God's divine plan for your life, then I would remind you of 2 Timothy 2:22, *"Flee also youthful lusts."*

Many teens today believe that anything short of sexual intercourse is okay. This is *deception*. It is shocking to know we live in a society where young girls are dared by their "friends" to perform oral sex in the back of school buses, and even more shocking to realize they are doing it. Could this be because society has tried to convince us that oral sex is not "real sex"?

CHANGING SEXUAL MORALS

In 1998, President Bill Clinton claimed he did not have sexual relations with Monica Lewinski. He claimed that oral sex was not technically having sex. While his accusers didn't buy his argument, unfortunately many young people did. At the time all of this was happening, according to a poll taken in the 1999 fall issue of *Seventeen* magazine, of 723 male and female teens between the ages of fifteen and nineteen, 49 percent considered oral sex inferior to sexual intercourse; 40 percent said that it did not count as sex. Nearly twenty years later, the "norms" for sexuality have advanced to a level that has cost thousands of people their lives, and infected millions more with sexually transmitted diseases. Add to that millions of innocent babies that have been aborted and you have what would normally be called a national crisis. Sadly, in our modern era, this is not considered a crisis. It is called "the new normal," and the church stands alone as the final beachhead upholding God's standard for sin and immorality.

Sexuality is God's gift to you. You must protect it and fight for its purity! Ezekiel 23:3 says, *"They committed harlotry in their youth; their breasts were there embraced, their virgin bosom was there pressed."* Ephesians 5:3 emphasizes that believers should not even allow a hint of sexual immorality to plague their lives.

Even though premarital sex is not a biblical option for Christian singles, some resort to skirting the rules—heavy petting, making out, vulgar dancing, fondling, and having sex with clothes on. You are progressing in the wrong direction. What do you expect the end result to be? There is no need to frustrate yourselves sexually. Don't even go there!

Unfortunately, our society often holds a double standard that says boys will be boys, and that girls must discern sexual temptations. The following is a list of the seven lines that boys typically say to girls to pressure them to engage in sexual activity before marriage:

1. "If you really loved me, you would."

2.   "Everybody's doing it."

3.   "I'm so excited, I can't stop."

4.   "You will not get pregnant."

5.   "If you get pregnant, I will marry you."

6.   "We're going to get married anyway."

7.   "Nobody will ever know about it."

If Satan can persuade young women into believing just one of these lies, he has robbed them of their purity and sexual integrity. In a 2014 study tracking the first wave of millennials to become parents, a team from Johns Hopkins University found that 64 percent of mothers gave birth at least once out of wedlock. Almost half of them had all of their children without ever exchanging vows. An article reporting on the study stated that these results were consistent with a separate study from 2012, which found that, among women under thirty, more than one-half of all births happened outside of marriage.[2]

If we don't instill the beauty and sanctity of sex within marriage into our sons and daughters, who will? The pressure to go along with the crowd is greater than ever. The need to fit in and be liked at any price can cause a lifetime of regret.

Even though we live in a hostile environment externally, we must constantly renew our minds in God's Word and guard our hearts from evil. It's easy to compromise in little ways that, in reality, are more harmful than they seem.

There is nothing wrong with having fun or wanting to be attractive to the opposite sex, but you must learn to protect yourself from destructive relationships that are born out of lust.

BEWARE OF SEXUAL SIGNALS

Ladies, one of the areas you must avoid is wearing suggestive clothing. The weakness of every man is a woman's body. When putting your clothes on, you know exactly what kind of reaction and effect it will have on men. With food, it has been said that presentation is everything; the same is true for the body. Dressing fashionably and attractively is different from dressing in a way that flaunts your body as if you are sending out a sexual invitation. Things have certainly changed from a few years ago. Now, it is not unusual to see a Christian

2. Jordan Weissmann, "For Millennials, Out-of-Wedlock Childbirth Is the Norm," *Slate*, June 23, 2014, http://www.slate.com/articles/business/moneybox/2014/06/for_millennials_out_of_wedlock_childbirth_is_the_norm_now_what.html (accessed August 10, 2017).

woman strolling down the street wearing a short shirt and low rise jeans just to show off her belly button ring.

The way you dress teaches people how to treat you. You teach the opposite sex to respect you or to disrespect you by the attire you wear. First Timothy 2:9–10 teaches women to *"adorn themselves in modest apparel, with propriety and moderation…but, which is proper for women professing godliness, with good works."* If that voice on the inside whispers, *This neckline is too low, That skirt is too short,* or *Those jeans are too tight,* you should listen. Let the redeemed of the Lord dress so, not just say so!

And, men, don't allow your eye to be the gateway to the lusts of the flesh. It's impossible to avoid being exposed to all the temptations out there, but you can stay away from situations that may cause you problems. Be aware of the TV you watch and the Internet sites you view. Protect your mind from access to improper images. Premarital sex only appears to be free of strings attached. But, in reality, it leads to addiction, sexually transmitted diseases, unwanted pregnancies, marital problems, and infidelity.

The cost of running sexual red lights is very high. You must balance the outward power of the world's hostilities with an inward thrust of moral conviction and dedication. First Thessalonians 4:3 says, *"For this is the will of God, your sanctification: that you should abstain from sexual immorality."* The word *abstain* means "to willfully hold back."

Who Jesus is, as told through your life, your posts,
and your viewing habits, is on display for everyone
who follows you and knows you are a Christian.

You can measure what kind of Christian you are by the cost you are willing to pay. What is your Christian life costing you? What do your social media posts and interests reveal about who you are in Christ? What does it say to the world, even to those few people who follow you, about Jesus? It costs something to guard your tongue. It costs something to dress modestly and to monitor the TV shows, movies, and music you listen to. It will cost you when you choose to miss out on all the "so-called" fun that everyone else is having because what they're doing violates God's will.

In this age of digital media, with instant access to *anything* with complete anonymity, we have to guard our integrity more diligently than ever. Our witness is at stake. Who Jesus is, as told through your life, your posts, and your viewing habits, is on display for everyone who follows you and knows you are a

Christian. We live in a society where anything goes. I want to ask you a question. Do you find yourself doing things you feel the need to hide? (See 1 John 1:6.) If you're hiding things from your parents, like social media posts, text messages, books, or movies that you would be embarrassed to talk about at church, then you are stepping into the darkness to do things you're ashamed of in the light.

GOD REDEEMS AND RESTORES

Maybe you are reading this and you already feel like damaged goods because of things you have done in your past. You feel that no respectable man would want you. You may feel as though you have to give men what they want, or nobody will want to date or marry you. You may have given in to temptation and now you don't know how a "pure" Christian man will accept you.

I assure you that God has destined someone to love you. Rest assured that they are living and breathing right now somewhere on this planet. They are going to love God and you passionately. Your job is to trust God and from this day forward keep yourself just for that special someone God will send to you.

God is a matchmaker! When He ties the knot in a relationship, it will hold—if you don't pick at the knot. Ecclesiastes 4:12 says that a threefold cord is not easily broken. You can't afford to have a twofold cord, which is a relationship committed just to each other. You must have a threefold cord relationship: you, your mate, and God intertwined together in a loving relationship.

According to the Bible, *"there are eunuchs who have made themselves eunuchs for the kingdom of heaven's sake"* (Matthew 19:12). To be a eunuch is to be sexually inactive. You can approach your sexually inactive single years in one of three ways: you can be a griper, a grabber, or a gripper.

Do you gripe all the time because you're not married or, depending upon your age, because you're not dating as much as you think you should?

Or are you a grabber? You will grab hold of anyone you can date or marry, regardless of reputation. You're like the old maid who was praying under a tree asking God for a husband, when she heard an owl in the tree saying, "Whoooo, whoooo!" She replied, "Anybody, Lord. Anybody will do!"

Anybody won't do! Don't be a griper or a grabber—be a gripper. This is someone who firmly grips hold of God's purpose. God said that it was not good for man to be alone, so, most likely, it is His will for you to marry. You may ask, "What about Paul?" He was single, yes, but unless you've given yourself so fully to God's work that you have no desire to be married, then God has someone for you when the time is right. You may not understand now, but God's timing is perfect.

To the man or woman contemplating marriage, I would ask, "What are your dreams? What goals have you set for yourself that you want to achieve before marriage?" You need a firm grip on God's purpose for your life. You need to use this time of waiting as a time of preparation. If you are half a person, you will attract half a mate. Quit attracting halves and start attracting wholes. It's all about His timing! Use this time alone to grip hold of God's plan for your life. Do you have emotional baggage you need to unload? Do you have your finances in order? Take advantage of this time to prepare yourself for marriage.

Note two things about the first marriage in Genesis. First, God knew what kind of mate Adam needed; and second, it was God who brought Eve to Adam. It is not unrealistic to believe that if you will wait on God and be sexually pure, then He will bring the right mate to you when the time is right. Don't waste valuable time until then.

Several years ago, I spoke to 24,000 teenagers in Knoxville, Tennessee. The message I preached became one of my most requested. It was entitled, "Keep Your Underwear On!" Exodus 28:42–43 tells us about what the high priests who came into God's presence, were to wear, *"You shall make for them linen trousers to cover their nakedness; they shall reach from the waist to the thighs"* (verse 42). Beneath the white robe, he was commanded to have "his underwear on." No matter how religious the priest looked outwardly in his priestly robe, if beneath his religious garb he did not have his linen britches on, then God would not allow him to live in His presence. In essence, the priest had to have sexual integrity in his private life.

Outwardly, many people have perfected their religious image. They look one way on the outside, but in private, they are someone else. First Samuel teaches, *"Man looks at the outward appearance, but the LORD looks at the heart"* (1 Samuel 16:7). If you want to live in the presence of God and have His favor on your life, then you must "Keep Your Underwear On!"

Don't believe Satan's lies of deception when he tells you that it is not possible to remain sexually pure until marriage.

I waited until I was twenty-five to get married. I was a virgin, and my wife was a virgin. Don't believe Satan's lies of deception when he tells you that it is not possible to remain sexually pure until marriage. We were both virgins. Today we have five children, so obviously we have made up for all those years of abstinence!

When Cherise and I started dating it wasn't long until we began to fulfill the Scripture, *"Greet one another with a holy kiss"* (Romans 16:16). It became our favorite verse. As our relationship progressed, we fell deeply in love. After we were engaged, we felt we needed to fulfill another Scripture as soon as possible, *"It is better to marry than to burn with passion"* (1 Corinthians 7:9). We even moved up the wedding date.

Naturally, as you begin to date, the relationship develops and there will be different intimacies reserved for each stage of the relationship. Understand that there are some intimacies reserved for friendship, others for courtship, and others reserved only for engagement. Of course sexual intercourse is reserved for the confines of marriage only.

I realize you are not going to walk up to someone and say, "Hi, Bob, I'm Jean. Let's get married in six months. I'll see you at the altar." First, you go through a growing and bonding process. What you must guard against is allowing a level of intimacy that is not sexually legitimate to cross over into relationships where they do not belong.

First Thessalonians 4:3–6 says,

> *For this is the will of God, your sanctification: that you should abstain from sexual immorality; that each of you should know how to possess his own vessel in sanctification and honor, not in passion of lust, like the Gentiles who do not know God; that no one should take advantage of and defraud his brother [or sister] in this matter,*

Paul was saying that you should not arouse sexual desires in another person that you cannot righteously satisfy. I know that when you love someone and plan to marry and spend the rest of your life together, it is hard to walk away when the desire for each other is so strong. But trust me, it can be done.

WHY SHOULD YOU MAINTAIN YOUR SEXUAL PURITY?

1. SO YOU WON'T SHAME THE NAME.

Samson fell to sexual sin, and the Philistines made sport of his God. (See Judges 16:23–25.) When we compromise our sexual integrity, we drag the sacred name of Jesus through the mud. We've all seen this happen, particularly when moral failure is exposed in the clergy.

2. SO YOUR WITNESS WON'T BE DISCREDITED.

This sin cripples your testimony to all the people to whom you have witnessed. It will discredit your witness because what you were offering did not work.

3. SO YOU WON'T CONTRACT SEXUALLY TRANSMITTED DISEASES.

Today, not only are preachers preaching abstinence, but doctors and health experts are warning that multiple sexual partners can cost you your life—or that of your loved one!

If at any point you discern an alarm going off in your spirit saying, *Warning! This isn't right,* you had better listen to it. God put that radar there. You may have ignored it in the past, but from now on, you should listen to it.

Don't repeatedly ignore the voice of discernment inside of you, or you may become desensitized to real danger. Remember, nobody can guard your body and your sexual purity but you. Defending your virginity is your responsibility.

I want to drive home the fact that if you are single and sexually inactive, you are not a freak! If you will be God's best, He will send you His best!

How many times have you read those infamous headlines at the supermarket checkout lines? "Learn to Please Your Man!" "Lose Weight in Ten Days!" "Be Happy!" On and on, the media plays on "surefire" ways to help women become happier, stronger, and more successful in life. Millions of dollars are spent on advertisements geared specifically for women who feel less than adequate in one or more areas of their lives. I don't have a problem with magazines promoting good health or lifestyle improvements for women; I just hate the fact that so many women are not finding out the truth about who they are and what they possess.

Beauty is good, and much appreciated by men. I thank God that I have a beautiful wife; but, more importantly, I thank God that I have a discerning wife. Real beauty comes from within, just as real happiness comes from within. Proverbs 31:10 asks the question, *"Who can find a virtuous wife? For her worth is far above rubies."* Her husband can safely trust in her. She will do him good and not evil all the days of her life. (See Proverbs 31:11–12.)

Ladies, in order for women to achieve all the things you desire—beauty, health, happiness, success, and good relationships—you must know the truth about how to achieve these things. It is not by achieving the ultimate dress size or learning how to please a man. No, the way to achieve all you desire is to become the woman God created you to be. Focus on pleasing Him.

Men, what is on the inside is far more important than what is on the outside. Beauty is vain; it will fade away, but the inner beauty of a discerning woman will live on. She will leave a legacy long after she is gone. *"Her children rise up and call her blessed; her husband also, and he praises her.... Charm is deceitful and beauty is passing, but a woman who fears the LORD, she shall be praised"* (Proverbs 31:28, 30).

Take a moment now to stop and reflect on what you have read, and what it means to you and for your life. Consider each of the questions below and journal your answers. Date this page, so that when you look back, you will have a record of your journey in this season of life. Any time the Lord speaks to you, it is important to record it.

DATE: _____

CHAPTER 14 QUESTIONS:

1. List two key points that were discussed and then give your understanding for each of those key points.

_____

_____

_____

_____

2. In chapter 14, the statement was made: "Don't believe Satan's lies of deception." Explain your understanding of the word *deception*.

_____

_____

_____

_____

3. How have you experienced Satan's deception in your life?

_____

_____

_____

_____

4. What do your social media posts say about the Jesus you represent?

_____

_____

_____

_____

5. What do your social media and internet searches reveal about your character?

_____

_____

_____

_____

6. What lies about yourself are you struggling with right now?

_____

_____

_____

_____

7. Based on what you have learned in this chapter, are there any areas of your life in which you will begin to act or think differently?

_____

_____

_____

_____

CHAPTER 14 CONCLUDING REFLECTION

Your reflection should include the following:

+ What you learned

+ What had the most value for you or had direct application to your life

+ Any other takeaways

_____

_____

_____

_____

_____

_____

_____

_____

_____

_____

_____

_____

_____

_____

_____

_____

_____

_____

_____

_____

15

DISCERNMENT TO WIN YOUR FAMILY

Believe on the Lord Jesus Christ,
and you will be saved, you and your household.
—Acts 16:31

Have you ever noticed there are more women in the church than men? More and more, women are finding it necessary to become the spiritual leaders of their home. More often than not, it is the wife who first encounters God, then, hopefully, the husband follows in her spiritual footsteps. It is the rare case when the husband is on fire for God and the wife elects to stay at home.

What do you do when you have an experience with God before your mate does?

In Judges 13, we read about a case of marital, parental, and spiritual incompatibility. Samson's father, Manoah, was a passive, laid-back, low-key person. The name *Manoah* actually means "rest." There is nothing wrong with a mild-mannered man who has a calm temperament. However, this Scripture indicates that he was also low-key and laid-back concerning spiritual things.

Manoah's wife was one of the nameless women in the Old Testament. All we are told about her is that she was sterile and remained childless for a long period of time until an angel of the Lord appeared, not to Manoah, but to his wife. God informed her that she would have a child, and instructed her to follow the rules imposed on those who made a Nazarite vow—a disciplined life with strict rules of diet and hygiene. (See Judges 13:3–4.)

It is significant that the angel appeared, not to Manoah, but to his wife. The angel informed her directly rather than going through her husband.

How should a woman handle it when God speaks to her first? What do you do when your man is laid-back and low-key about spiritual things and you are not? What do you do when you are excited about Jesus, the church, and the Word of God, but he seldom wants to go to church or discuss spiritual matters? It's tough when you come home from church excited about what the Lord is doing in your life, while your husband is snoring on the couch, or out hunting, or watching sports on TV.

Spiritual incompatibility is a real problem for many couples. It affects the relationship on all levels. It is a great area of testing for many marriages, and it takes a wise woman to know how to handle this challenge.

INCITE SPIRITUAL JEALOUSY

Manoah's wife is a perfect example of a woman whose marriage was incompatible on several different levels. She had a spiritual encounter with God before her husband did. Then the angel of the Lord gave her specific instructions about how to raise her son, Samson. Manoah and his wife experienced parental and spiritual incompatibility.

Samson was to be raised a Nazarite. The Nazarite vow was an act of consecration. The person taking this vow was to avoid anything from the vine (no wine), could not touch anything that was dead, and was not to cut his hair until the resolution of the vow. This child was to be separated and isolated for God's use. He would live a restricted lifestyle that would require great discipline. In order to raise a child according to the Nazarite vow, the father and mother both had to be extremely committed. As sure as Manoah's wife was of what God was telling them, Manoah was left in the dark. (See Judges 13:2–24.)

How do you raise kids to live for God when their father doesn't live for God? This woman had a son whom she wanted to set apart for God's call, but the father was oblivious to God's will.

Instead of acting independently or maneuvering to get her husband to do what was required, she was patient with her husband until Manoah finally prayed a powerful prayer:

> O my Lord, please let the Man of God whom You sent come to us again and teach us what we shall do for the child who will be born.   (Judges 13:8)

How do you raise your kids to live for God when only one of the parents is a believer? Manoah's wife gives us a fine example. She wasn't ugly to her husband; she didn't move out of their bedroom because he didn't share her faith. She didn't badger her husband, or compare him to "So-and-so's" husband, who was so spiritual. She simply communicated what God had said to her and, as hard as it must have been, waited for God to speak to him.

What makes you think God can't speak to him? I don't care if he has cotton in his ears. I don't care if he gets drunk or high, God can speak to him.

Let me encourage you to pray this prayer:

God, I know he's not spiritual right now, but speak to him. He needs to know how to raise our children, so speak to him. God, as the priest of our home, I need him to cover me spiritually. Speak to him on the job or in his sleep. Speak to him in his car or in the shower. Speak to him through circumstances and through other people. But please speak to him!

Manoah's wife had an awesome revelation about how God wanted to use her son, but her husband was out of the loop. When she told him what the angel had told her, he wanted to have the same experience she had. There was something about this woman that provoked her husband to spiritual jealousy. She didn't provoke him to anger, nor did her encounter with God provoke him to frustration. If she were always moaning and complaining and wore her discontent on her sleeve, why would Manoah have wanted any part of that? Instead, she lived out her faith in such a way that it provoked her husband to spiritual jealousy—he craved what she had.

Spiritual jealousy, inspired by the life his discerning wife modeled before him, lit a fire in Manoah for the same spiritual relationship with God that his wife enjoyed. Live your life so that your husband will want what you have. Let him observe how gently you treat him, when you could have embarrassed or cut him down. A holy life will produce the deepest impressions.

In 1 Corinthians 7, Paul had advice for the lone believing spouse:

But to the rest I, not the Lord, say: If any brother has a wife who does not believe, and she is willing to live with him, let him not divorce her. And a woman who has a husband who does not believe, if he is willing to live with her, let her not divorce him. For the unbelieving husband is sanctified by the wife, and the unbelieving wife is sanctified by the husband; otherwise your children would be unclean, but now they are holy. But if the unbeliever departs, let him depart; a brother or a sister is not under bondage in such cases. But God has called us to peace. For how do you know, O wife, whether you will save your husband? Or how do you know, O husband, whether you will save your wife? (verses 12–16)

Live your life in such a way that your husband will:

+ Feel the warmth of your sweet spirit

+ See the joy of the Lord in your life

+ Feel loved as you pour respect and honor into him

MARRYING THE ILLUSION

The real world of marriage is not always peaches and cream. The problem is that we marry illusions. It seems God has a sense of humor because He doesn't always give us the illusion we wanted. For example, you looked at that man before you were married and you envisioned him attending church with you, holding the Bible in his hands, and leading the kids in devotions at night—so wonderful and spiritual and sensitive.

But after the honeymoon, the only time he goes to church with you is when someone is *hatched* (baby dedication), *matched* (wedding), or *dispatched* (funeral). He's a CEO Christian—Christmas and Easter only.

Men can marry illusions as well. You imagine coming home from work to the sight of your beautiful wife waiting at the front door with your bedroom slippers and silk robe.

She asks, "How was your day, darling?"

You answer, "It was torture."

Then she says, "Kiss me, you fool," as you fall into one another's arms and begin to rip off each other's clothes.

Nice fantasy; but it's not real life.

Another illusion is the physical illusion. They say love is blind, so you don't see any of the physical flaws while you are dating. But a few years after you are married, you begin to notice all of his physical imperfections. His belly is hanging over his belt, he burps after meals, and he snores in bed. Or, your once perfect, swimsuit-model wife has packed on some pounds, she doesn't always wear make-up and do her hair, and she snores something awful as well!

You stare at the person lying next to you and wonder, *What did I marry?*

After the violins stop playing, and the bubbles have burst in the heart-shaped Jacuzzi, sometimes you feel real pain the next morning. Your marriage will not always pan out like the soap opera, *Days of Our Lives*. These are the "days of your life," when you must reach beyond romance to responsibility, beyond sex to sensitivity. This is where the highway can become littered with casualties who signed up for marriage without fully realizing what they were signing up for.

You didn't marry a Hollywood star. This is a real man or woman, from the crown of his or her head to the soles of his or her feet. Maybe he's no Prince Charming. Maybe she's no Sleeping Beauty. He might not be as spiritual or as romantic as you wish, but he's yours! She may not be your mother in the kitchen or your fantasy in the bedroom, but she's yours! If you don't want to face the devastation of divorce, you need to make it work.

Ladies, there are not many good men around—you better concentrate on what you have! You can't read *Esquire* and *Cosmopolitan* and win this battle. Oprah can't tell you how to have a successful marriage because she's never been married herself.

Gentlemen, there probably isn't a long line of women just waiting to grace you with their presence. Appreciate the one who is there on the sidelines, cheering you on.

Ladies, there are some things you just should not do in public. I don't care how ADD he is, I don't care if he's got his entire foot in his mouth, don't embarrass and belittle him publicly. If he gets his words mixed up, if he makes a mistake, stand right there by his side and grin as though he could do no wrong. Afterwards, in the privacy of your car, you can discuss it if you feel the need.

Gentlemen, your wife is a reflection of you. Her countenance will be a reflection of how you treat her. Treat her with disrespect, contempt, and shame, and that is how she will appear. Treasure her as your queen, and your queen she shall be. You can't mistreat her at home and expect her to shine in public. She's not that good an actor.

DISCERNING INTIMACY

Some think that being a Christian means that we have to be offended at anything sexual. Many unsaved men resent the church because it turns their wives into a holier-than-thou "church lady." Before they were saved, the marriage and sex was great. She wore pink lingerie to bed, and sex was wonderfully creative! But now that she's born again, she wears a granny gown and sleeps with a Bible lying on her bosom. Whenever he makes advances towards her, she says, in a religious, stained-glass voice, "Touch not God's anointed."

That may be a humorous image, but when it's time to be intimate in your marriage, if you're lying in bed speaking in tongues, he's wondering, *What has that church done to my wife?*

Make him jealous of your spirituality, not resentful of it. For too long, the church has been a haven for disgruntled women whose lives are out of balance.

God created sex for marriage. Married couples learn how to please each other; singles learn how to please the Lord. If you are married, your first ministry is to your spouse.

Scripture says, "*Do not deprive one another except with consent for a time, that you may give yourselves to fasting and prayer; and come together again so that Satan does not tempt you because of your lack of self-control*" (1 Corinthians 7:5). That means that the sexual relationship in a marriage should be so frequent that you only refrain from sex for a short time of fasting and prayer. Then as soon as the fast is complete, you get back to business! Consistency is important; don't give Satan an opportunity to tempt you with unfaithfulness.

YOUR MARRIAGE ASSIGNMENT

When you and your spouse are spiritually incompatible, it's easy to become frustrated and build up bitterness and resentment. If you will roll into his arms instead of rolling toward the wall or if you will cook him his favorite meal when he least deserves it, then you are planting seeds into his heart that will cause him to want what you have spiritually. Manoah's wife decided to make her marriage work even though she and her husband were spiritually incompatible.

What she desired was for God to show her husband their assignment— His eternal purpose for this couple being together. God wanted them to raise Samson as the champion who would deliver God's people.

Allow me to press in and ask a few tough questions for married couples living in the real world, with all its challenges and temptations. Today, with the touch of a screen on your phone, you can find just about any immoral, deviant sexual image or video your mind can think of. There are literally no limits, and no one else will ever know about it. How are you dealing with this? Are you leading a secret life? Let me ask an even harder question. Do you experience guilt and feel like a failure when you give in to temptation and go places on the internet you wished you hadn't? To be honest, if you are going to these sites and not experiencing any guilt, then I doubt the reality of your salvation, because one of the roles of the Holy Spirit is to convict you of your sin. But even if you *are* feeling guilt, remorse, and shame when you stumble, is that really how you want to live your life? If this behavior was revealed or discovered, is this really how you want your children to see you? Do you really want to live a life of secrecy and deceit? Do you really think it won't lead to an affair or the destruction of your home and marriage? Is this really the legacy you want to bring before God on that great judgment day? Do you really think the only one you are affecting is you?

Every marriage has an assignment. God didn't put you together just to have sex, a house payment, and a two-car garage. When you enter the kingdom of God, you receive an assignment. Your children have a divine assignment, and the enemy wants to abort it. That's why infidelity and divorce are so devastating; they not only affect the husband and the wife, but they also destroy God's assignment for the entire family.

> *Every marriage has an assignment. God didn't put you together just to have sex, a house payment, and a two-car garage. When you enter the kingdom of God, you receive an assignment.*

It's hard to come home to an unspiritual man. It's hard to raise your children according to God's Word when your mate is not saved. Manoah's wife shows us, when you're living with a man who is not spiritual, you can provoke him to spiritual hunger.

Finally, the angel of the Lord appeared to Manoah, too. After this visitation, he went to his wife and asked for further instructions. If your mate is unsaved, don't talk to him about spiritual things all the time. Sometimes discernment means being quiet until God gives you the opportunity to speak. At the right time, God will give you a chance to talk. When that door opens, ease on in. "*The wise woman builds her house, but the foolish pulls it down with her hands*" (Proverbs 14:1).

Psalm 68:6 says, "*God setteth the solitary in families: he bringeth out those which are bound with chains*" (KJV). The word *solitary* means "single," in reference to a single diamond, a precious jewel. In other words, I believe God hovers over families, and He finds one single, solitary diamond in every family. He sovereignly picks one member of the family to deliver those bound with spiritual chains.

Do you know why God saved you first? You are His beachhead—God's entry point, God's doorway—through which He will reach the rest of your family.

Manoah and his wife raised Samson. They fulfilled the assignment of God upon their family. Samson grew up and became a mighty deliverer of God's people.

Many years ago, my personal assistant at the time, Susan, was the first to be born again in her family. For two years, she attended church alone. Every Sunday after church, she went home to her husband and her twenty-year-old son, who did not share her faith. Her husband, Alan, was a good man and a good provider. He just was not interested in spiritual things. Sunday was his day to drink beer and play golf.

Often, Susan would leave the atmosphere of praise and worship at church and go home to her husband and son who were totally unspiritual. Many nights she cried herself to sleep, wondering if her family would ever be saved and share her faith.

After two years of coming to church by herself and living for God alone in their home, the Holy Spirit began to speak to her about how to win her husband. He challenged her to control her tongue. As she began to show Alan respect, honor, and unconditional love, slowly his heart began to melt.

She prayed Ephesians 1:17–18 for him, every day:

That the God of our Lord Jesus Christ, the Father of glory, may give to you the spirit of wisdom and revelation in the knowledge of Him, the eyes of your understanding being enlightened; that you may know what is the hope of His calling, what are the riches of the glory of His inheritance in the saints.

She was winning him without saying a word. Her gentle, kind spirit was witnessing to him.

As Alan watched the change in his wife, he started attending church with her in September 1993. Even though he was not converted immediately, every Sunday he attended church with Susan.

Tracy, their twenty-year-old son, observed his father going to church week after week with his mother. On October 3, 1993, Tracy decided to check out church. That Sunday morning, Tracy walked down the aisle, was born again, and filled with the Holy Spirit.

A few weeks later, on October 31, I preached an illustrated sermon, where Tracy played one of the characters. When I gave the altar call that morning, Alan walked down the aisle and was gloriously saved and filled with the Holy Spirit.

God had an awesome assignment for this family. Tracy began to exhibit extraordinary leadership gifts. Several years later, he became a successful children's pastor in our church. Today, he leads the teams at Free Chapel as Executive Pastor and helps us minister to thousands of people weekly through all of our campuses and ministries.

Over the years, Satan had tried to convince Susan that her family would never be saved, but this discerning woman kept on praying and loving. She was patient and kind to her husband. She knew God had an assignment for her family, and she would not give up until God brought it to pass.

What assignment will you abort if you give up on your family? Acts 16:31 says, *"Believe on the Lord Jesus Christ, and you will be saved, you and your household."*

God has set you as a solitary diamond in your family to deliver those bound with chains. Like Manoah's wife, you are going to see God's assignment for your family come to pass.

Take a moment now to stop and reflect on what you have read, and what it means to you and for your life. Consider each of the questions below and journal your answers. Date this page, so that when you look back, you will have a record of your journey in this season of life. Any time the Lord speaks to you, it is important to record it.

DATE: _____

CHAPTER 15 QUESTIONS:

1. List two key points that were discussed and give your understanding for each of them.

_____

_____

_____

_____

2. Give a brief summary of your reading from chapter 15:

_____

_____

_____

3. Describe how the voice of God spoke into your life in chapter 15:

_____

_____

_____

_____

4. Based on what you have learned in this chapter, are there any areas of your life in which you will begin to act or think differently?

_____

_____

_____

_____

5. Do you feel equipped to lead your family? Why or why not?

_____

_____

_____

6. If you knew God was calling you to equip yourself at a greater level, would you?

_____

_____

_____

7. What are three ways you could grow in your family relationships?

_____

_____

_____

_____

CHAPTER 15 CONCLUDING REFLECTION

Your reflection should include the following:

+ What you learned

+ What had the most value for you or had direct application to your life

+ Any other takeaways

_____

_____

_____

_____

_____

_____

_____

_____

_____

_____

_____

_____

_____

_____

_____

_____

_____

_____

_____

16

A LIFE WORTH REMEMBERING

She has done what she could…Assuredly, I say to you,
wherever this gospel is preached in the whole world,
what this woman has done
will also be told as a memorial to her.
—Mark 14:8–9

Ask yourself, A hundred years from now, will it even matter that I was born? Are the things I'm living for, worth Christ dying for?

In the *Guinness Book of World Records*, I read about a man who eats glass, metal, and wood. He has eaten ten bicycles, a supermarket cart, and seven television sets. But the most astonishing reason he will forever be remembered is because he ate a Cessna light-flying aircraft, after grinding it up and mixing it with his food. That's how he spent the fifteen most famous minutes of his life.

Imagine him standing before God one day. The Lord asks him, in a baritone voice, "What did you do with your life?"

His only answer, "I ate an airplane!"

How will you be remembered? What kind of legacy are you leaving for your family?

WHAT CAN YOU DO?

The Gospels tell of a woman who lived a life worth remembering. Jesus was dining at the home of Simon the leper when a woman approached with an alabaster jar of costly perfume. She broke the jar and poured the perfume on Jesus' head and feet. Lovingly, she wiped the perfume from His feet with her hair, weeping as she did so. Jesus, aware of what was to come, accepted it as His anointment for burial. (See Matthew 26:6–13; Mark 14:3–9; Luke 7:36–48.)

Others who were present, including the disciples, were bothered by this. Some questioned the waste of expensive perfume when it could have been sold and the money given to the poor.

In Luke, it says that she "*stood at His feet behind Him weeping; and she began to wash His feet with her tears, and wiped them with the hair of her head; and she kissed His feet and anointed them with the fragrant oil*" (Luke 7:38). In that one verse is a list of five things that she did for Jesus, and they all regard His feet.

+ She stood at the feet of Jesus.
+ She washed the feet of Jesus.
+ She dried His feet with her hair.
+ She kissed His feet.
+ She anointed His feet.

Jesus was so moved by this woman's passionate worship, that He forever immortalized her, "*Wherever this gospel is preached in the whole world, what this woman has done will also be told as a memorial to her*" (Mark 14:9).

Her life became memorable not for the things that she couldn't do, but for the fact that "*she* [did] *what she could*" (Mark 14:8). God will never ask you to do what you can't do. If He asks you for something, it just means He's already put in you the ability to do what He's asking. Don't insult God by telling Him you can't do it.

This woman not only did what she could, but she also did it in the face of criticism. Jesus' host for the evening, a Pharisee, said, "*This man, if He were a prophet, would know who and what manner of woman this is who is touching Him, for she is a sinner*" (Luke 7:39).

Imagine her shame and embarrassment as, while she was washing Jesus' feet, others in the room called her a sinner. This was not news to her. She knew that. Isn't it amazing how many people will criticize you when you start to do something for Jesus? Her critics attacked her. They accused, "What you're doing is a waste." Still, she did what she could.

STRENGTH IN BROKENNESS

In the 1950s, Paul Anderson was the strongest man in the world. He was able to carry 6,270 pounds on his back.

Once he was asked, "Were you ever a ninety-pound weakling?

He replied, "Yes, when I was four years old."

One day at church, Paul was moved to give his life to Christ while hearing a quadriplegic man give his testimony. How about that? The strongest man in the world was won to Christ by one considered to be among the weakest. God used the weakest man He could find who was willing to do what he could do.

Many people will never live a life worth remembering because they are not willing to be broken—they want to strut.

For God to use you, you will have to pass the praise test and the criticism test. How do you pass these tests? You learn to give the praise and criticism you've received to God. Jesus immortalized this woman because of her extravagant worship. He was moved when she broke open the alabaster box of expensive oil to anoint His head and feet.

"We have this treasure in earthen vessels" (2 Corinthians 4:7). You and I are the earthen vessels, and the treasure on the inside is our worship to God. If people are going to know about your love for Him, there must be brokenness. Just as the alabaster box was broken, we too must be broken, in order to offer Him praise. Many people will never live a life worth remembering because they are not willing to be broken—they want to strut. You don't have to be a super achiever or have a great IQ. You don't have to be amazingly talented. All you have to do to be used by God is to be broken enough to pour out your love on Jesus. If, in doing so, you get an inroad to win one soul, then you will have lived a life worth remembering for all eternity in God's eyes.

LIVES WORTH REMEMBERING

I want to salute some men and women who are living lives worth remembering:

1. I SALUTE THE FATHERS AND MOTHERS WHO STICK WITH THEIR CHILDREN THROUGH THICK AND THIN.

In John 18:25, the most famous mother in the world is standing at the foot of the cross, while her precious son is being crucified.

In the midst of dying, Jesus tenderly instructs John the beloved to take care of his mother. Mary was present when He was born, and she was present when He died. She was there to console her son in His darkest hour. Men try to act grown, but if they get in real trouble, they want their mother's comfort. Jesus was no different. In His hour of trouble, He wanted His mother near. It had to be very difficult for Mary to see her son precede her in death.

Often, people are who they are because they had praying parents or grandparents in their lives. Some of you reading this book have parents who chose to have you instead of pursuing great personal success. They could have gone to college themselves, but they paid your tuition. They could have retired by now or could be living a better lifestyle, but they made some tremendous sacrifices to help you do things they've never done or go places they've never been. Children don't always appreciate the enormous sacrifices their parents have made to ensure a better way of life for them. I want to commend every mother and father who have stood by their children in the good times and the bad times.

I want to warn you not to love your children to death. Sometimes we can love our children so much that we are practicing borderline idolatry. You have to discern when you love your child to death instead of loving your child to life. When you let them talk to you disrespectfully without disciplining them, you love them to death, instead of loving them to life. Some people don't prepare their children for the harsh realities of the real world. When we don't show our children tough love at times when discipline is necessary, we can actually be sowing seeds of rebellion into our kids that make them think rules don't apply to them.

You can go overboard in sacrificing yourself for your kids. When you love them to the point where you don't want anyone else to spend time with them, you're going overboard with your love. When you feel nobody is good enough to marry them or date them because you're so picky, your obsession with your child is hurting them, not helping them.

Love your children, support your children, and stand by your children, like Mary did on her Son's toughest day as He went to the cross. Never give up on your kids. Love them to life, not to death.

2. I SALUTE MOTHERS, FATHERS, AND CHILDREN IN NONTRADITIONAL FAMILIES.

I also want to salute the mother who did what was best for her child, even if it meant giving him up for adoption. Not everyone will have agreed with your decision, but at least you had the courage to birth the child rather than abort him. It took courage to release the child into a loving, stable family.

Moses' mother hid him for three months because of Pharaoh's decree to kill all male children two years old or younger. I'm sure it was a difficult decision to send her crying infant down the Nile River in a basket. She was forced to give up her baby. Adoption is a very sensitive issue. Millions of women have had to give up their children by force or by choice, trying to do what is best for their children.

As teenage pregnancies continue to rise, some high schools are designated only for children who are pregnant. When I was growing up, if a girl became pregnant, her academic career was pretty much over. She was forced to drop out of school.

Today, the family is being redefined. Millions of children are living in homes that don't fit the stereotype of what a traditional family is supposed to be.

Just because you're a single-parent family doesn't mean your family can't function well in the sight of God. On the other hand, just because you have a perfect home setting with a two-parent family does not mean you have a wonderful home life.

The ideal family setting is two parents: mom and dad raising their children together. I remember reading in the Bible about a traditional family that had two parents. The mother was a homemaker, the father was a farmer, working by the sweat of his brow, and they had two children. They had everything their hearts desired; they didn't want for anything. However, they ended up homeless, forced to live in the streets. In a domestic violence dispute, one of the sons killed his brother.

The parents were Adam and Eve, and their sons were Cain and Abel. According to the standards of the world, they were the perfect family, living in the perfect environment. Yet they still became a very dysfunctional family.

Don't allow family pain or shame to hold you hostage to the past. Moses' mother had to give her child up, not because she didn't love him, but to save his life! Maybe you were adopted and raised by one parent, a grandmother, or some other relative. You were given up for adoption. As a result, feelings of worthlessness may flood your emotions. Why would my mother or father give me up? Perhaps like Moses' mother, yours did what she had to do to save your life.

Moses' mother did what was best for her son. She knew that in her present condition, she couldn't give him what he needed. Pharaoh's daughter eventually adopted Moses. He lived in somebody else's house, not with his real mother. However, he lived a better life than he would have if his natural mother had raised him. Thank God for people who take children into their homes and invest in their lives by loving and treating the children as one of their very own. You're living a life worth remembering.

3. I SALUTE EVERY SINGLE PARENT WHO HAS RAISED CHILDREN ALONE.

In 1 Kings 17, we read the story of a widow and her child living in the midst of a famine. This single parent home was on a strict budget. Mother and child were down to their last meal.

Perhaps you have had to make tremendous sacrifices working two jobs or more, just to make ends meet while raising children all by yourself. You tried to do what was right in front of your children, doing it alone. Congress can't seem to balance the budget in Washington, DC. Perhaps they need to take lessons from the amazing single parents who live on a shoestring budget with kids to feed and clothe.

I salute you. You're living a life worth remembering.

In 1 Kings 17, the poor widow opened her house to the prophet Elijah. When he asked her to share some food from her meager rations, she explained her dire circumstances. Elijah then demonstrated the abundant resources of God for single parents who show faith:

And Elijah said to her, "Do not fear; go and do as you have said, but make me a small cake from it first, and bring it to me; and afterward make some for yourself and your son. For thus says the Lord God of Israel: 'The bin of flour shall not be used up, nor shall the jar of oil run dry, until the day the Lord sends rain on the earth.'" So she went away and did according to the word of Elijah; and she and he and her household ate for many days.

I want to salute the mothers who have been pushed out of the way. It is a hard pill to swallow, but it happens every day. When a man divorces his wife and leaves his kids from his first marriage, that doesn't make them just go away. Just because a man gets a new wife and a new family doesn't mean the old family doesn't exist.

Many of you may be in a similar situation. Somebody closed the book on you and rode off into the sunset. He can't do enough for his new family, but he has totally forgotten about you and your children. We're living in a society where it has become normal for people to get divorced and then move on like nothing ever happened. Men can get a woman pregnant and then just ride off into the sunset to become successful.

God, however, stands ready to protect you. If you will not become bitter, He will bless you and your children. Even if the child's father never blesses you, God will bless you! Lift your head up. Don't let anybody make you feel ashamed.

If you won't get bitter, God will be *"a father of the fatherless, a defender of widows"* (Psalm 68:5).

4. I SALUTE GRANDPARENTS WHO ARE RAISING THE CHILDREN OF THEIR CHILDREN.

I want to salute those of you who may not have given birth yourself to the kids you are raising, but you've taken someone else's children, perhaps your son's or daughter's.

It is estimated that over six million grandparents are raising their grandchildren as their own. Sometimes, because of their children's addictions or immoral lifestyles, grandparents with big hearts are opening up their homes and adopting their grandchildren. They are living a life of sacrifice by investing in the lives of their grandchildren as if the children were their own.

Just like the woman whom Jesus immortalized in Scripture, yours is also a life worth remembering.

DISCERNING THE PRESENCE OF THE SPIRIT OF JESUS

In Luke 2, Mary, Joseph, and their twelve-year-old son, Jesus, had been in Jerusalem for the Feast of the Passover. Religious activity had filled their days. Crammed full of what happened in the temple, they started their long trek home.

A day into their journey home, they noticed that Jesus was missing. Mary and Joseph frantically checked with all of the relatives in their party, but Jesus was not to be found.

Here's the lesson in the story of lost Jesus. While leaving a tremendous spiritual feast, Mary and Joseph lost the presence of Jesus. Traveling in a caravan with all their religious friends and relatives that had joined them in their religious exercise, suddenly it dawned on them—we've lost the personal presence of Jesus!

If there is one thing I want you to carry with you after reading this book, even if you forget everything else, it is this: you must be very discerning so as not to lose the personal presence of Jesus! You cannot take Him for granted.

When you're not in the temple, ask yourself, *Do I have His personal presence? Am I fellowshipping and taking Him into my home?*

Mary and Joseph had Jesus with them in the temple. They lost Him on the way home. Jesus doesn't just want to be in church. He wants you to have His personal presence in your home, and in your daily life.

Don't start for home and lose the personal presence of Jesus. The most unlikely person to lose Jesus was Mary, His mother. I question if anybody loved and understood Him as much as Mary did. She was in His inner circle, but Mary lost Him. How close she was to Jesus! Their very lives were interwoven together. He was part of her; she was part of Him. Yet she lost Him. Although you may get very close to Jesus, you must be very careful that you do not lose Him.

Not only did Mary lose Him, she didn't even recognize it. The Scripture said, *"Supposing Him to have been in the company"* (Luke 2:44). She thought He was there. Isn't that the danger with all of us? We take too much for granted. We don't do that in our businesses. We take nothing for granted, closely examining the books and balance sheets. But when it comes to our relationship with Christ, we get comfortable with merely assuming that He is in our company.

Notice that Mary and Joseph were among religious people when they lost Christ. Not only was she the most unlikely person to lose Him, not only did she lose Him and not know it, but she lost Him in the most unusual place. Where? Not at a theatre, casino, or a club; she lost Him in the temple among holy things, among holy surroundings.

Mary and Joseph lived three days without Him. When they finally found Jesus, they found Him where they had lost Him, in the temple. At first they blamed Him, but Jesus reminded them that He was in His Father's house—the temple—where they had left Him.

Where did the prodigal son find his father? Exactly where he had left him!

You'll find Jesus where you lost Him. If you'll only go back there, He's ready to forgive. *"I will heal their backsliding; I will love them freely"* (Hosea 14:4).

YOUR SPIRITUAL LEGACY

How will you be remembered? What kind of legacy are you building?

I pray that as you have read this book a new sensitivity to spiritual things has been activated in you. Your discernment has been awakened. You are a man or woman of purpose. You are equipped with a special gift from God to encourage and lift everybody to whom you are assigned. You will discern the hiss of the tempter, and you will recognize the still, small voice of God. Special promptings from the Holy Spirit will gently nudge you toward encounters with the right people in the right places at the right times, fulfilling the right plans for your life. I pray that your spiritual legacy will be worth remembering from generation to generation.

You have just read the final chapter of the book. Congratulations for finishing this journey. Take a moment now to stop and reflect on what you have read, and what it means to you and for your life. Consider each of the questions below and journal your answers. Date this page, so that when you look back, you will have a record of your journey in this season of life. Any time the Lord speaks to you, it is important to record it.

DATE: _____

CHAPTER 16 QUESTIONS:

1. List two key points that were discussed and then give your understanding for each of those key points.

_____

_____

_____

_____

2. Chapter 16 mentions "Strength in Brokenness." Can you see a broken part of your past or your life that the Lord is asking you to release so that He can make something beautiful out of it? Are you willing to release it to Him today?

_____

_____

_____

_____

3. Take a moment now to stop and reflect on all that you have read, and all that you have journaled. Please take a moment and go back and read your notes from each chapter. What stands out to you the most about what you have written in previous chapters?

_____

_____

_____

_____

4. As you look back over this book, take a minute to write about what parts have meant the most to you.

_____

_____

_____

_____

5. Please take a minute to reflect on your experience since you started reading *Right People, Right Place, Right Plan.*

_____

_____

_____

_____

CHAPTER 16 CONCLUDING REFLECTION

Your reflection should include the following:

+ What you learned

+ What had the most value for you or had direct application to your life

+ Any other takeaways

_____

_____

_____

_____

_____

_____

_____

_____

_____

_____

_____

_____

_____

_____

_____

_____

_____

_____

ABOUT THE AUTHOR

Jentezen Franklin is the Senior Pastor of Free Chapel, a multi- campus church. Each week his television program *Kingdom Connection* is broadcast on major networks all over the world. A *New York Times* best-selling author, Jentezen has written eight books including the groundbreaking *Fasting* and *Right People, Right Place, Right Plan*.

Having a passion to serve others and foster unity, he was awarded the Martin Luther King Jr. Mantle of Destiny Award for his work and efforts for racial reconciliation. Jentezen has served as an advisor to CEOs and business leaders of multiple organizations and is listed among notable alumni at Barton College in Wilson, NC. Additionally, he has served on an advisory board to the President of the United States.

Jentezen and his wife Cherise have been married thirty years, have five children and two grandchildren, and make their home in Gainesville, Georgia.

For more resources to help you grow, we offer online courses.
To find out more about these courses, go to jentezenfranklin.org,
click on GROW and then on COURSES.

May the Lord bless you as you continue to allow Him to develop you
for His purpose. It is my sincerest desire that you encounter the right
people, in the right places, with the right plan. Trust in God and He
will order your steps.